A Handbook for
School Governors

Second edition

More people than ever before are becoming school governors: parents, teachers, business people, and other members of the local community. This handbook, now in its second edition, provides a readable and comprehensive introduction to what is involved. The new edition has been completely revised to take account of the provisions of a number of important Acts in the 1980s, especially the 1986 and 1988 Education Acts, which have extended the role of school governors.

The authors, who have both run and contributed to training courses for governors over many years, describe the new responsibilities of school governors, which include greater control over the curriculum, conduct in school, financial running of the school, staff appointments, and communication with parents. They describe how committees work and give examples of tricky situations, such as pupil exclusion, accidents, or when a school is threatened with reorganization or closure. Practical and down-to-earth in their approach, they encourage school governors to be aware of the great potential their work has for improving the education of children in our schools.

The authors
E.C. Wragg is Professor of Education and Director of the School of Education at the University of Exeter. J.A. Partington is Senior Lecturer and Vice-Dean of Education at the University of Nottingham.

A Handbook for
School Governors

Second edition

E.C. Wragg *and*
J.A. Partington

Routledge

First published 1980 by Methuen & Co Ltd
Second edition by Routledge 1989
11 New Fetter Lane, London EC4P 4EE

Typeset by Photoprint, Torquay, Devon
Printed in Great Britain
by Mackays of Chatham PLC, Kent

British Library Cataloguing in Publication Data

Wragg, E.C. (Edward Conrad) *1938–*
  A handbook for School governors.
  1. Great Britain. Schools. Governors. Role
  I. Title II. Partington, J.A. (John A)
  379.1'531'0941

  ISBN 0–415–03803–0
      0–415–03804–9 (Pbk)

Contents

Acknowledgements

The authors and publisher would like to thank the following for permission to reproduce the material cited below:

Cambridge University Press for the extract from *Science Watch* by Paul Butler, David Carrington and Graham Ellis (1986); Macmillan London and Basingstoke for the extract from *English for Living* by A. Rowe (1976), for the diagram from *Changing the Primary School* by John Blackie (1974), and for the extract from *Your Language. Two*, by Maura Healy (1981); Grafton Books for the extract from *Royal Road Reader*, Book 1 (1970); Longman for the extract from *The Loose Tooth* by David Mackay, Brian Thompson, Pamela Schaub and Posy Simmonds (1970), and for the extract from *Nuffield Physics Year 1* (1978); Addison-Wesley Publishers for the extract from *Mathematics for Schools*, Level 1, Book 6, by Harold Fletcher *et al.* (1970); Ginn and Company Ltd for the extract from *Ginn Mathematics*, Level 7, Textbook 2 (1984); E.J. Arnold for the extract from *Tricolore* Stage 1, 1B by Sylvia Honnor, Ron Holt and Heather Mascie-Taylor (1980); Nelson & Sons Ltd for the extract from *Life in Our Society*, vol. 2, by K. Lambert (1975); Oliver & Boyd for the extract from the Schools Council Modular Course in Technology *Problem Solving Workbook*, published in association with the National Council for School Technology (1986); and Cambridgeshire County Council for the LFM budget of Buckden Primary School from *Local*

Financial Management, Peat, Marwick, McLintock (Longman, 1988).

They would also like to thank Caron Robinson for the chart on p. 8; Adam Yeldham for several cartoons in the text and Jonathan Hall for the cartoons on pp. 27 and 36 – the second of which is also the cover illustration.

Introduction

During the 1980s successive Acts of Parliament gave school governors not only more power but more responsibilities. At the beginning of the decade governing bodies were harmless and fairly subterranean and, indeed, did not even exist as separate entities for the many primary and secondary schools who had a single managing body, the local Education Committee. By the end of the 1980s governors had virtually become employers, particularly as a result of the 1988 Education Act.

This is a book for ordinary folk who find themselves elected, coerced, co-opted or even, for all we know, tricked by their crafty fellows into becoming a school governor. The contents are based on our experience as governors of schools, and from training sessions we have organized for school governors at our respective universities.

We have found over the years that governors' needs are fairly straightforward, and can perhaps best be indicated by giving some of the questions the new or established governor commonly asks:

- How can I help the school?
- Where can I find out more about what happens in schools?
- What is expected of me when I am appointed?
- I am a parent or teacher. How can I best serve the people who elected me?

1

- How does a committee work?

- What are governors supposed to do if a really tricky problem emerges?

- Where can we turn for help if we don't understand a particular matter?

- Can governors actually get something done?

We have used these questions as our guide when considering what to write about and how to divide our subject matter.

Some school governors will already be extremely knowledgeable in one or another field, and their expertise can usually be of great help to their less well-informed fellows, though on occasion it may be an obstacle to progress. Teacher governors will know a great deal about education in general as well as their own school in particular. People who have served on other committees will often be very knowledgeable about committee procedures. There may be lawyers, builders, doctors, social workers, bus drivers, mothers or factory workers on a governing body, all of whom know something useful about children, the community, buildings, rights and obligations, curriculum and social problems. Putting one's knowledge and experience at the disposal of one's fellows rather than blinding them with science is the hallmark of the successful expert, and the same applies at however modest a level to a school governor who offers something useful, be it experience as a parent or detailed knowledge of building regulations. The two most important qualities of the effective school governor are:

(a) A concern for the well-being of the children, teachers and others in the school community.
(b) Commonsense.

Given these two attributes in sufficient quantity amongst the membership of a governing body many problems can be solved.

Is being a governor a waste of time?

It is, sadly, the case that some governors' meetings are so tedious and unimportant they make Samuel Beckett's pause-laden *Waiting for Godot* look like *Ben Hur*. At the end members, their brains corroded beyond redemption, resolve to go home and do something really exciting, like counting the pages of the telephone directory.

Sometimes the sense of purposelessness occurs because none of the governors takes any interest in the school. The result is that when matters come up for decision only the head and the teacher representatives really know or care what is going on, and, being as human as the rest of us, feed in just as much information as is necessary to get the rest of the governors to support what they want. Although some heads and teachers prefer that governors should show little interest in the school, most much prefer it when governors take the trouble to inform themselves about what is on the agenda so that they can see all points of view.

It will be seen in Chapter 3, 'Being an effective school governor', that there is plenty of scope to help the running of your school. In some ways, the very title of 'Governor' is unhelpful, because it suggests that the holder is someone who gives orders to subordinates; it is perhaps this point of view which encourages antagonism on the part of some teachers. In practice governors give few orders as such: their function is less to control the school than to help to sort out problems and get the best possible deal for their school from all the outside agencies.

Several years ago when the Taylor Committee (set up by the Department of Education and Science) proposed increased powers for school governors the General Secretary of the NUT described the recommendations as a 'busybodies' charter' — an inflammatory statement, but one which illustrates how sensitive is the issue of control over children's education. In our experience the best partnership between professional teachers and interested lay people in the community, be these governors or parents, occurs when it is accepted that decisions about the day-to-day running of the school must be made by the paid professionals, but with proper regard for the views of the lay people concerned. There are countless examples of this mutual respect and trust working well, and rather fewer of it working badly.

On the other hand there is now a legitimate concern for accountability in education as in other spheres. Serious doubts have been expressed about the quality of education some children receive, and issues such as the teaching of basic skills, preparation for adult life, relevance, and standards of achievement are discussed endlessly in the press and at meetings.

Governors who take the trouble to inform themselves about life in school, and then use their energy and imagination to help the school will not be wasting their own time or that of anyone else.

The purpose of this book

Education has become such a vast and complex business that even those who spend their whole life in teaching cannot hope to be familiar with more than a small fraction of what goes on. Thus no governor, upon reading a single volume, can become an expert in all aspects of school government.

Our hope is that governors who take the trouble to read this book will be a little better able to do their job, will understand more clearly what goes on in schools, and will be able to play a full part in governors' meetings.

In Chapters 1 and 2, therefore, we concentrate on how governors fit into the educational system and what they are expected and empowered to do. Chapter 3 looks in more detail at the job of the individual governors, be they parents, teachers or LEA nominees, showing how they can make a contribution to the life of their school. It includes a section on training for governors. We turn to the question of governors' meetings in Chapter 4 explaining how committees work, the importance of group dynamics, and an analysis of dirty tricks (a topic rarely discussed in texts on the subject).

Chapters 5 and 6 are about life in school and current issues in education. It is, of course, impossible to do more than prick the surface of these topics in two chapters, but we hope that reading them will give governors an appetite for discovering more about the problems of learning and teaching in our schools.

Finally in Chapter 7 we analyse some thorny issues which often perplex governors when pupil suspensions, accidents or vandalism are discussed, or when the school is reorganized or threatened with closure.

An optimistic/realistic view

Our principal belief is an optimistic one: that most governors are trying to be helpful. We realize, of course, that some are not, and that certain governors may even be arch-villains, enemies of humanity, but we believe that few come into this category.

4

Similarly we believe that most teachers work hard for the good of their pupils. We have both visited hundreds of schools throughout the country, worked in several on a regular or occasional basis, and trained thousands of novice or experienced teachers. We have some knowledge of teachers or heads who do give cause for concern, and of schools where all is not well. In general, however, we find most teachers deeply concerned for their pupils' welfare and learning.

We concentrate, therefore, on trying to encourage a *positive* partnership between interested governors and professionally committed teachers and heads, whilst knowing that this will not always occur because we are talking about real human beings, with all their frailties, not identikit Hollywood heroes.

We hope that people reading this book will find education as interesting as we do ourselves. We have both attended our share of conferences where sombre-faced educators proclaim gloom and doom, and have read our fill of papers on education which call toys 'learning stimulus materials'. We have minimized the professional jargon so that interested lay people can read the book for pleasure not penance, and if certain descriptions are in a lighthearted vein, that is because human behaviour in general, and events in school or committees in particular are often funny, pretentiousness and pomposity being especially hilarious.

Three points are worthy of mention. First of all no book about education can be comprehensive or completely up to date. A change in government or in LEA policy can reverse a situation which has operated for years. We describe situations as they are at the time of writing. Thus we address sections of the book to parent, or teacher governors not because of any favouring of some group, nor in anticipation of legislation, but because governing bodies have several categories of governor. However, all are equally governors, sharing a common interest in the good of the school. We have included the most up to date information about the effects of the 1988 Education Act available at the time of writing.

Secondly, we concentrate on primary and secondary schools in the state system. Much of what we describe will be relevant to colleges of further education, special, denominational or independent schools, but our principal focus is on primary and secondary schools. It would need much more space than we have available to describe adequately the issues covered in all our educational establishments.

5

Thirdly, we have adopted the convention of using sometimes 'he' and sometimes 'she' when writing about governors, heads, teachers or pupils in the singular. The impression could otherwise be given that all key positions are held by men.

Finally, governors of schools in Scotland and Northern Ireland will find some variations in practice from what we describe, which is the current situation in England and Wales. These differences are, however, often only slight.

1

How governors fit into the educational system

When governors are appointed it is difficult for them to know how they fit into the national, regional and local system. 'What powers do I have?' 'How am I supposed to do what Parliament and the LEA expect of me?' 'Does the Department of Education and Science ever come into it?' are amongst several questions asked by newcomers, or even by established governors when they find the powers, responsibilities or duties of governors being discussed or reviewed.

Who's in charge?

This is probably the most difficult question of all on the education system of England and Wales. The basis is a type of power-sharing: no single person or body has supreme authority, but rather a large number of individuals and organizations are consulted, involved and given responsibility for parts of the system. Even the Secretary of State for Education and Science, the 'top' person in the system, appointed by the Prime Minister and occupying a seat in the cabinet, has only limited powers, and the Education Act of 1944 gives him only the somewhat vaguely defined task of 'promoting the education of the people of England and Wales', though the 1988 Act gave him more powers.

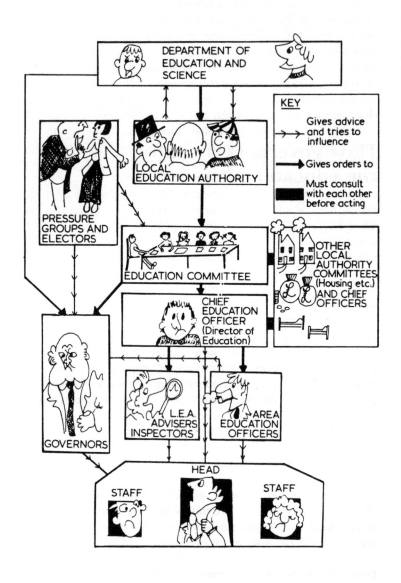

Figure 1 'Who's in charge?'

8

This intentional sharing of influence and authority is the envy of educators in countries which have more authoritarian governments, and just as much the despair of enthusiastic British reformers who, having been granted a glimpse of their paradise on earth, cannot find the right levers to pull to bring it about. 'You want me to be a dictator,' lamented one Secretary of State when challenged as to why something of which his questioner disapproved had not been put right.

Figure 1 shows the educational system in simplified form. In some cases instructions are given by superiors to subordinates, and these are shown by bold arrows. For example, the Education Committee of your Local Education Authority,* in trying to carry out the wishes of the electorate, lays down policy guidelines which must be followed by you as governors, and equally by the Chief Education Officer or Director of Education as he or she is sometimes called, the senior employee in the authority's education department. Under the Education Acts of 1980, 1986 and 1988 Parliament lays down the areas of school life with which governors must be concerned and for which they are responsible.

Just as important are individuals and groups who advise and bring all sorts of influence to bear: these are indicated by the light arrows. Pressure groups are nowadays very active in several fields. Some, like parent-teacher associations (PTAs), are local in origin, others like CASE, the Confederation for the Advancement of State Education, are national. Many are set up to promote particular causes only to disappear again when the cause is achieved or dead. Some of these attempt to have old schools replaced or outside toilets scrapped; denominational groups will be formed to support schools of their own persuasion. In recent times some groups have campaigned to stop the closure of village schools. It is thus an important part of the system that everybody should have an opportunity to talk to everybody else, and that as many people as possible are brought into the decision-making process. It can be slow, but it often works well.

How a local education authority works

It used to be the case that the local authority sub-committees set

* The local education authority is the County Council (in non-metropolitan counties), the Metropolitan District Council (in metropolitan counties), the London Borough Council (in London).

up for various purposes (for example to look after roads, education, welfare, housing and so on) worked more or less independently of each other. Each received an annual allocation of public funds and set about spending it as it pleased. The work of these sub-committees often overlapped: e.g. the people planning new housing developments needed to know of decisions made by the committee in charge of siting new schools: for one to act without the other was wasteful.

People began to argue that it was not the best use of public funds to have one department designing and building council houses and another, quite separately, designing and building schools. Clearly they had much, if not everything, in common, and both of them needed also to be in touch with the authorities concerned with fire prevention. Nowadays, too, the legislation affecting employers in their relationships with employees has become so complex that a separate personnel officer is often necessary to oversee the position amongst all council employees, including teachers and other employees of the Education Committee. Last but not least, a council may decide in one year to spend less on education but more on welfare. It may even be necessary sometimes to divert money at short notice from one sub-committee to another, and a particular project in education may have to be stopped.

It is with a view to providing a constructive solution to these and other problems of communication and consultation that many local authorities have introduced what is called *corporate management*. The effect is that the various committees must work more closely together. Furthermore, the Chief Education Officer is but one member of a Chief Officer's Committee, which can collectively review decisions and if necessary ask him or her to think again. The leader of this powerful committee, known as the Chief Executive, is directly responsible to the county council. This sort of consultation is shown in Figure 1 by broad bold lines. In short it means that even a Chief Education Officer is not always in the position to give you what you want, however much he may wish to, and however hard you lean on him.

What do all these bodies do?

The Department of Education and Science does not send out detailed instructions about how schools should run on a day-to-day basis, though Education Acts such as those passed in 1980, 1981, 1986 and 1988 have to be implemented, so it does have a responsibility to the government of the day to see that the government's wishes are carried out and that public money is wisely spent. The DES effectively influences the system through its control of finance. Its permission must be obtained, for example, before schools can be built or adapted. It has often been argued that this financial power gives the DES excessive influence, and there have been occasions when it has, albeit under political pressure, refused permission to build comprehensive schools for 11- to 18-year-olds or tertiary colleges. In the same way the DES has a profound effect on the supply of teachers into the system, through its influence over the numbers of teachers admitted to training institutions.

The DES regularly issues to the local education authorities various papers. The most potent of these are departmental regulations (officially called *statutory instruments*), and they are part of the law of the land, covering a range of subjects from school buildings to student grants. Less authoritative are the so-called *circulars* which are meant to reveal current DES thinking and call for consultation. The spirit of these is one of 'This is only a suggestion, ladies and gentlemen, but *do* remember who is making it!'

These circulars have been known to have far-reaching effects over many years. Indeed, comprehensive reorganization was initiated by a circular, number 10 of 1965, which indicated for the first time that the DES and the government were becoming interested in the actual organization of schools, a matter which had hitherto been the sole responsibility of local authorities, and many LEAs were initially outraged that the DES was seeking to interfere in the running of schools. The next government issued Circular 10 of 1970 which appeared to put the responsibility back with local education authorities. Finally, there are the *administrative memoranda* which, as the name suggests are concerned with smaller, day-to-day matters.

From time to time also the DES invites independent reports on parts of the education system. There have been many of these during the last thirty years or so, and ideas produced in them have found their way into schools and the system. Some of the most significant ones appeared in the 1960s: the Robbins report on higher education (universities and polytechnics), the Crowther report on the education of 15- to 18-year-olds (sixth formers), the Newsom report on the education of children who intended to leave school as soon as possible, and the Plowden report on primary education. Cynics argued that these reports appeared in exactly the wrong order: there might have been more logic in starting with primary education, rather than finishing with it.

Of particular interest to you as a school governor was the 1977 Taylor report on the management of schools entitled *A New Partnership for our Schools*. It proposed radical changes in the way schools should be governed. All such DES-sponsored reports are purely advisory. It is up to the government to decide whether to give their recommendations the force of law. At another level it is for LEAs and individual schools to discuss how recommendations can, or should be implemented. You should follow press coverage of such reports as they will often be in the minds of teachers for a two- or three-year-period.

Lastly, on a quite different front, the DES has the legal authority to make decisions over disputes which cannot be settled amicably 'further down the line'. It can happen from time to time that the other parties to the system – governors, parents, LEAs – disagree and dig in their heels. The parties are entitled to appeal to the DES for a ruling, which, when given, has the force of law.

Usually the DES tries to work through reason and persuasion, and brings out its heavy artillery only when some major issue of principle is involved. Even here, though, the powers of the DES are more restricted than used to be thought. In 1975 the Secretary of State for Education and Science ruled that the Tameside Local Authority was acting 'unreasonably' in going back on a scheme for comprehensive schools in its area which had already been agreed with the DES. When Tameside Local Authority challenged the Secretary of State in the High Court, the judges ruled in turn that Tameside was after all acting reasonably. In the eyes of the law, the DES could not rule that the Authority was acting *unreasonably* if what it really meant was only that it *disagreed* with Tameside.

You will probably have already noticed how often the term '*reasonable*' has been used, and it is characteristic of the way our education system works. It is assumed, rightly or wrongly, that governors, parents, teachers and administrators will work together harmoniously, with the DES as senior partner.

The local education authority provides and runs schools, makes sure that sufficient school places are available, and employs teachers accordingly. More than half of the necessary money comes from local ratepayers, and the rest from the government in

12

the form of the annual Rate Support Grant. Needless to say, each side wants the other to pay more, a favourite quarrel being the issue of teachers' salaries, which the local authorities sometimes wish to be paid entirely by the government. In theory, local education authorities can do what they want with their own money: the government money comes with policy strings attached.

During the last few years there has been an increase in earmarked government money for such matters as in-service training for teachers, non-advanced further education and special initiatives such as the support of small schools or the introduction of a new examination such as the General Certificate of Secondary Education.

Different types of school

Voluntary schools

Voluntary schools are the direct descendants of schools which were going concerns before Parliament began to take an interest in education in the late nineteenth century. Although the original buildings, sometimes substantially modernized, may still be in use in many places, there are also many new buildings which have been erected since the 1944 Act. Originally the schools were self-supporting through fees from parents and income from charities and endowments and bequests. As time went by these schools found that they also needed government money to survive, and the government started subsidies to them in 1833. Since 1902 the responsibility for aiding these schools from public funds has rested with the LEAs. Since a local authority nowadays has no choice but to provide school places for all children who need them, it is usually very ready to include voluntary schools in its planning for the area, as a cheaper alternative to building its own.

You may find, then, that your school is not owned by your local authority, but by an educational trust or charity, or possibly by one of the bigger religious dominations. Somewhere among the dusty files in the clerk to the governors' office there will be a document called a Trust Deed which, along with your Articles of Government, may well lay down conditions as to how the school is to be governed, and you should make sure you know what these are. It is just not possible here to mention all the things you might find. Most common, perhaps, will be the requirement that the school should teach the Anglican or Roman Catholic faith; possibly you will have to take in children from a particular area, and so on, depending on the intentions of the people who originally drew up the deed and provided the original endowment.

There are nowadays three types of voluntary school, of which the *voluntary aided school* is the most distinctive. In such a school you and your fellow governors are responsible for seeing that the outer fabric of your school is well maintained and decorated and for paying the bills for this — although at present 85 per cent of this money will be refunded to the school by the DES. Similarly, if the decision is taken to enlarge the school, or perhaps even to move it somewhere else, which often happens (say from a city centre to a green belt site), then, as before, you will have to see that the builders are paid and the 85 per cent reclaimed.

A *voluntary controlled school* probably started its life as something very akin to a voluntary aided school, but has found that it cannot keep up its financial commitments. As a result, the local authority will have taken over all the financing of the school, and will also have become for all practical purposes the employer of the staff, as in its own county schools. The task of governing the school will be much more like that of governing a county school, although there may still be some additional provisions to observe in the trust deed.

There are also in existence 131 *special agreement schools*. These were established as a 'one-off job' in the later 1930s, and local authorities paid between 50 and 75 per cent of the cost of establishing them. None has been set up since, nor are any more likely to be established, and the functions of the governors and their duties are very similar to those of voluntary aided schools.

Governors of all voluntary schools are also required to co-operate with the local authority in the medical and dental inspection of pupils, and in the School Meals Service. Usually this entails making such premises and equipment available at the school as the authority requires.

Finally, the Articles will give you some say in the admission of pupils to the school. Since the school is an integral part of the local authority's plan for the area, the actual numbers in the school will be agreed with the authority. However, an Anglican school would clearly give preference to Anglican pupils, and so on.

Schemes of local financial management (p. 27) will apply to voluntary schools.

CTCs, as they are usually called, are a new type of school introduced by the Education Act of 1988. The government intended that there should be about twenty such schools in the country as a whole from Plymouth to Newcastle-upon-Tyne. The first one opened in Solihull in 1988.

These schools have several novel characteristics. In a bid to involve industry more with the running of schools, it is the intention that City Technology Colleges should be set up in the first place by donations from industry and then, like the 'grant-maintained' schools described later in this book, be maintained by funds paid directly from the DES. The CTC grant bears some relationship to what the LEA spends on its secondary schools in the area.

A tricky area is whether the LEA should provide the usual 'support services' to CTCs — the schools' psychological service, training courses for teachers and so on. LEAs do not normally supply such services to independent schools, and CTCs are officially classified as independent. If no agreement is reached with the LEAs, the Secretary of State may have to raise his grant to enable CTCs to 'buy in' what they need.

CTCs are 11–18 comprehensive schools taking their boys and girls 'wholly or mainly' (1988 Act) from the area in which the school is situated. Their curriculum has a distinct emphasis on science and technology. For this reason it was intended that both pupils and parents should demonstrate a readiness to take advantage of the type of education offered in CTCs. It is this characteristic which produced some accusations that CTCs would inevitably turn into selective schools.

From the point of view of school management, it is interesting to note that CTCs are independent schools but with a difference. Their individual agreements with the Secretary of State, for example, oblige them to carry out his wishes in many respects. The Secretary of State may vary national agreements about working conditions and wages and salaries for all the different employees of CTCs. The CTCs are, however, open to inspection by HMI.

The Education Act of 1988 says nothing about the governing bodies of CTCs. As CTCs are set up as charitable trusts like other independent schools, they have both a group of trustees (doing roughly the same job as that of foundation governors in voluntary schools) and a governing body, which will no doubt be tailored to the local needs of each CTC. It is likely that industrialists will play a leading, if not dominant, role.

Grant-maintained schools ('Opted out')

This too is a new category of school set up by the Education Act of 1988. Such schools have acquired the popular title of 'opted-out' schools. Briefly, a way was opened for governors and parents to choose to cut the link between their school and the LEA. If they do so, they will take over the entire management of the school and will be financed directly by the DES. This is in some respects similar to the 'direct grant' system of financing schools which was phased out in the 1970s.

Only schools with more than 300 pupils may 'opt out'. To do so, the governors must hold a secret postal ballot of parents. Governors can decide themselves by a simple majority vote whether to ballot parents about opting out. If the initiative comes from the parents rather than the governors, however, it must have the written backing of '. . . a number of parents of registered pupils at the school equal to at least 20 per cent of the number of registered pupils at the school'. If such a request comes from the parents, governors cannot refuse to hold a ballot. The DES will pay the costs of the ballot. The decision to hold a ballot must be agreed at two governors' meetings held no fewer than 28 days and no more than 42 days apart.

'Opting out' is clearly a momentous step to take. Parliament was concerned that it should not be taken lightly, and for that reason governing bodies which conduct a ballot must see to it that the full implications for the school of 'opting out' are spelled out to parents at voting time. If less than 50 per cent of registered parents vote in the ballot then the governors must arrange a second ballot within 14 days of the results of the first ballot being known. The second ballot is then binding and a simple majority decides the outcome, even if few people bother to vote.

If the final ballot shows that parents of pupils at the school want to 'opt out', the proposal goes to the Secretary of State for approval, in the same way as other proposals for the reorganization of schools. The Secretary of State can approve it, turn it down or approve it with some modifications. We can only guess why a proposal might be turned down. The Secretary of State might take the view that so few parents bothered to vote that there was really not enough interest in 'opting out' to make the new school a success. Perhaps the majority was too small. The Act talks of 'a majority' only – a majority of one seems hardly enough. The Secretary of State must also listen to any objections made to him about the proposals. One could imagine that the LEA objections might arrive in an asbestos envelope! Other schools could be affected by a school 'opting out' and they too can object to the Secretary of State. Alternatively a school which is judged by the LEA to be too small to be viable might be refused grant-maintained status by the Secretary of State, especially if he is under pressure from the Treasury to reduce expenditure and sees the non-viable school as too expensive for him to bail out.

It is hard to give examples of why governing bodies might wish to 'opt out'. Press reports suggest that some county schools faced with reorganization resulting from falling rolls might 'opt out' in the hope of retaining their cherished sixth forms. Other enthusiastic governing bodies may simply feel that they could make a better job of running their school's financial and educational affairs than the LEA.

It is important to remember that the freedom of action granted by 'opting out' is not infinite. Fees to pupils cannot be charged, for example, nor can such schools become academically selective. The fear has been expressed that 'opting out' was intended by the government as a way of reintroducing selection at 11+. 'Opted out' schools must keep the same educational character as before. Moreover, the grant to be paid annually to an 'opted out' school will be broadly in line with what the LEA previously spent on the school, so there are no obvious financial advantages.

The governing body of an 'opted out' school consists of:

5 elected parents

1 or 2 (but no more) elected teachers

The headteacher

Enough additional governors to outnumber those already mentioned. If the school was formerly a county school, these will have the new title of 'first' governors. If the school used to be a voluntary school, the established title 'foundation governors' will be used. At least two 'first' or 'foundation' governors must be parents of children at the school when they are appointed.

Who can be a governor?

The 1986 Education Act required quite specific categories of people to be represented on school governing bodies:

* *Parents of children at the school.* They are elected by a properly organized secret postal ballot.
* *Representatives of the LEA.* They are usually councillors, but an LEA can nominate anyone to represent it.
* *The headteacher* can decide whether or not to be a governor. It depends largely on whether the head sees herself as the governors' chief executive or a member of the board of directors as it were. Whatever the head decides to do she is entitled to be present at all governors' meetings.
* *Teacher governors* are elected by their colleagues.
* *Co-opted governors* are elected by the rest of the governing body. Among the co-opted governors should be what the Act calls 'members of the local business community'.
* *Foundation governors* exist only in voluntary aided and voluntary controlled and independent schools (see p. 14).

The latter are often but not always church schools and are usually schools created years ago by benefactors who left or gave sums of money to 'found' schools. Nowadays foundation governors are appointed separately to look after the interests of the foundation. In practice this means that they decide how the foundation money or assets of the school shall be managed, and they usually have separate meetings from time to time for this purpose. The day-to-day running costs of the school, by far the biggest contribution, comes of course from the LEA, but the existence of foundation funds gives the governors some degree of independence from LEA policy. Some foundation funds are very small indeed, others may run into millions.

Appointment to be a foundation governor depends very largely on how the foundation is run. Anyone interested in becoming such a governor could get in touch with the clerk to the foundation governors who may be a different person from the clerk to the main governing body, to which all the schools' governors belong.

Governors other than foundation governors normally serve for four years. A teacher governor who leaves the school must resign

as a governor when she leaves, but a parent governor can continue
for the four years even if her child is no longer in the school.

Who cannot be a governor?

Don't bother to try to become a governor if you are declared
bankrupt: the regulations do not allow it. If you agree to pay your
debts in full you must wait five years from the date of the
bankruptcy agreement before you can become a governor. If the
bankruptcy ceases you can become a governor (again) straight
away, of course.

The same applies to criminal convictions. If within the
previous five years you have been sentenced to at least three
months without the option of a fine, you cannot stand as a
governor. Moreover, if you have been fined for creating a
'nuisance and disturbance on educational premises' as the Local
Government (Miscellaneous Provisions) Act of 1982 puts it, you
are also disqualified. Curiously, the Regulations say that the
'disturbance' conviction must be for an offence 'at the school', so
it looks as if you can quite happily beat up the school next door
where you are not a governor! You may even occasionally meet
people who think that merely by being a governor you are
'creating a nuisance and disturbance on school premises'.

Do not think, by the way, that you can just sit tight and say
nothing if these disasters strike. You are required by law to write
to the clerk and confess all, though the regulations say nothing
about what might happen if you don't.

You will also automatically cease to be governor if you fail to
attend meetings without consent for a continuous period of
twelve months. Your fellow governors, or whoever appointed
you, can put you back in office (if they can remember what you
look like).

No one under the age of 18 at the time of appointment or
election may be a governor. This rules out the hitherto growing
practice of having pupil governors, elected by the pupils of the
school, who, in some cases, spoke far more sense than their older
fellow governors. However the rules say nothing about the
presence of pupil *observers* at governors' meetings. If governing
bodies choose to go down that road, however, great care must be
taken to draw up principles of procedure and confidentiality in
consultation with the clerk to the governors and to stick to them

19

rigidly. In particular there should be clear guidelines about what should be discussed in the presence of observers, and what not. The legal consequences of failing to do so could be very nasty indeed, both for individual governors and relationships within the school. The same applies if governors decide to go into 'open session' and invite the public and press. In such cases the agenda must be divided into unreserved (public) and reserved (private) business.

It is a very helpful development in the 1987 Regulations that no-one may be a governor of more than four schools at the same time. Schools benefit greatly from having a governing body whose members are devoted uniquely to that school and in which members do not have conflicts of interest with governorships of other schools. Government policy during the 1980s has sought to give each school its own governing body, and sharply to reduce the possibility of having several schools 'grouped' under one governing body. It is thought-provoking that until the early 1980s at least one LEA had one governing body for all its fifty-odd secondary schools. Each meeting consisted of head teachers queuing in a waiting room to appear in turn before the panel, read their report, be questioned briefly and then leave.

How are governing bodies made up?

The 1986 Act lays this down in great detail. It depends both on the type of school and its size.

Schools with fewer than 100 pupils
    2 parents
    2 LEA nominees
    1 teacher
    1 headteacher
    3 co-opted governors (A voluntary controlled school has 2 foundation governors and 1 co-opted governor.)

Schools with 99–299 pupils
    3 parents
    3 LEA nominees
    1 teacher
    1 headteacher
    5 co-opted governors (A voluntary controlled school has 4 foundation governors and 1 co-opted governor.)

20

Schools with 299–599 pupils
   4 parents
   4 LEA nominees
   2 teachers
   1 headteacher
   5 co-opted governors (A voluntary controlled school has 4 foundation governors and 1 co-opted governor.)

Schools with more than 599 pupils
   5 parents
   5 LEA nominees
   2 teachers
   1 headteacher
   6 co-opted governors (A voluntary controlled school has 4 foundation governors and 2 co-opted governors.)

The composition of governing bodies for the new grant-maintained ('opted-out') schools and for City Technology Colleges is slightly different and is described in the sections of this book about those types of school.

Although the numbers increase with the size of the school, the underlying principles do not change, and there is some subtle thinking behind them. The first point to notice is that the largest single group of governors is the 'co-opted' group which indicates that they will wield considerable influence if they feel united on an issue. The remaining governors – who elect the co-opted governors – have, therefore, a considerable interest in who is co-opted. Since the co-options are likely to be made at the first meeting of a new governing body, attendance at that meeting is likely to reach an all-time high. Moreover, it will not be possible for the teacher, parent or LEA governors to dominate the co-option proceedings, since none of these groups holds a voting majority over the other two.

On the whole these changes are beneficial. LEAs who may wish to keep a tight rein on their governing bodies through representation on it will find it difficult to do so – although the crafty ones might try to ensure that the party faithful whose support can be relied on stand for election as parent or teacher governors. If this strategy succeeds, then we may find that the co-opted members are chosen for their political interests rather than for their interest in the school, and this would be a pity. When Lord Joseph was Secretary of State for Education he invited comments from the public before the 1986 Education Act was drawn up. The powerful representation of party political members was one of the most criticized aspects of previous governing bodies.

On the positive side, the present composition of governing bodies should bring about more constructive discussion about the school between the various groups represented, because no single group dominates; each needs the support of the others to carry the day. This should go a long way to stopping what the authors feel is the unhelpful practice of caucus meetings beforehand where members decide on strategy or voting. At one time these were commonplace among LEA representatives and there were signs that parent and teacher governors were picking up the same bad habit. This book is written in the belief that a governor is a governor wherever he or she comes from. Everyone's concern is the interest of the school as a whole, not of sectional interests.

The chair and vice-chair are elected at the first meeting of the year, unless the Articles of Government for your school say otherwise. Anyone who works at the school — say a teacher, secretary or groundsman, cannot be chair or vice-chair. Nor can a pupil at the school, even if over 18. Apart from these limitations every governor is eligible. These two positions are discussed later in this book, but it is vital that people of goodwill should volunteer. If you are new to governing bodies, by the way, beware of politically motivated members who try to seize these positions by prior planning. The chair and vice-chair are often proposed and seconded in the first seconds of a meeting before some members have even collected their thoughts and opened their papers. It is only afterwards that people discover it was a hi-jack planned at a political caucus meeting. Insist on a proper discussion about the type of person needed before falling for this trick.

2

Governors' responsibilities

They say that if the guards on British Rail trains insisted on carrying out all their responsibilities each time a train pulled into a station, such as checking the wheels, balancing the load evenly across all carriages and so on, no train would ever run. If the full list of governors' responsibilities looks too formidable, remember that commonsense decrees that schools too must be allowed to run and that no individual governor is expected to live on the premises trying to organize the school singlehandedly. The head and teachers are the professionals charged with that daily responsibility. Do not resign your governorship just yet, therefore. See how it goes for a year first.

Whereas the LEA has to deal with many schools in its area, the governing body and the head of the school are responsible for one school only. The practice of grouping several schools under a single governing body, common at one time (see p. 20), is now severely limited, since it is clearly the intention of Parliament to work towards a situation where each school has its own governing body. LEA can still 'group' two or more schools, but the agreement of the governors must be secured first, and all the parents and teachers in the group must be allowed to take part in the election of their governors. Moreover, the Secretary of State has to agree to the 'grouping', except where the group is to consist of two primary schools only. There may be sense in having a common governing body where two schools work closely together, say a junior school and a nearby infants' school which sends most of its children to the junior school. However, it may be just as effective to have one or two governors who serve on both bodies.

On your appointment as governor you should be given a document containing the Articles of Government for your school. If you are not, then the clerk to your governing body should be able to find you one fairly quickly.

Although some of the document will be of necessity couched in rather dull and legalistic language, it is worthwhile to persist with those sections which refer to the conditions under which you hold office as a governor, and the powers and duties you have.

It is important to remember at all times that it is the governing body *as a whole* which has power to do things and *not* individual governors acting on their own. This is why the Articles always refer to 'governors' in the plural. The intention is in no way to squash your keenness or willingness to help as an individual, but rather to see that authority is exercised properly by the group, not by an individual.

It would be wrong, for example, for a parent governor to seek to use his position to secure preferential treatment for his own child at the school, or for a politically appointed governor to seek to have supporters of his party appointed to the teaching staff. For this reason, anything the governing body wishes to do must be decided by a resolution at a meeting. None of this applies to friendly and informal visits to the school which can usually be arranged by talking to the headteacher. Indeed, it is through such amicable contacts that you can become a trusted and respected member of the school community, and discover the ways in which you can best help.

Since the mid-1970s school governors in primary and secondary schools have been given far more responsibility than ever before. At one time their work was given to them by the LEA, and it must be said that they were not really a force to be reckoned with. Many LEAs tended to keep major decisions about 'their' schools largely to themselves and give governors only minor matters to decide. Others delegated more important matters to their governors but at the same time saw to it that they (the LEA) kept a strong voting majority on governing bodies, which ensured that governors were unable to get up to anything of which the LEA disapproved.

In the 1980s, however, Parliament and the DES started to lay down nationally what tasks governors should undertake and generally to intervene in school government by insisting that governors' powers and duties appear in the Articles. Inevitably this has become a political issue, with some people protesting that LEAs are being stripped of power and that local democracy is under threat, while others argue that democratic control is coming down to school level from County Hall, and that in this way local government is becoming even more local.

The major documents which governors should know about are:

The Education Act 1980

The Education Act 1981

The Education (No. 2) Act 1986

The Education (School Government) Regulations 1987 (SI 1987/1359)

The Education Reform Act 1988 (this is the Act of Parliament which in passing was called the 'Great Education Reform Bill' and GERBIL for short)

These can all be borrowed via the local library or bought for a few pounds, though most governors will prefer to consult summaries provided by their LEA or those given in national newspapers and magazines, or in specialist education papers like *The Times Educational Supplement* and *Education*.

Legislation and regulations about governing schools are raining down thick and fast these days and even LEAs sometimes have difficulty keeping up with them. None of this could possibly be described as light bedtime reading, but the clerk to the governors should have access to copies if the need should ever arise for governors to consult an Education Act. Do not hesitate to look up what an Act says, rather than being content with being told.

Governors' duties

Governors' duties are described by each LEA in the Articles of Government for your school. However Parliament has laid down the minimum duties of governors which must be included in the Articles, and these are outlined briefly below. Before going on to these, however, it is necessary to understand the responsibilities of the headteacher.

The Articles always say that the headteacher is employed to be responsible for the 'internal organization, management and control of the school and shall exercise supervision over the teaching and non-teaching staff'. The fundamental principle has always been that the head and his staff are the acknowledged experts on how to teach. In practice this means that the headteacher's advice and experience of the school must be very carefully considered at all times: while the headteacher does not have a veto on what governors choose to do, it would be foolish indeed under normal circumstances to press on with any matter if the consequences which the headteacher has explained suggest the opposite.

There are good reasons why the headteacher should be given ultimate control over the internal workings of the school. Not only is he the experienced senior professional, but the efficient running of a school requires a series of on-the-spot judgements; if every decision had to be referred back to the governors chaos would result, since for most of the time they are not present and governors' meetings usually take place only once or twice each term.

It is however not unreasonable for the governors to ask the head about decisions he has made since the last meeting, and, moreover, the head is required by the Articles to report certain matters to the governors — when pupils are sent home for disciplinary reasons, for example. The price the head pays for the high degree of discretion guaranteed him by the Articles is that he alone is responsible if anything goes wrong through internal mismanagement. The head's discretion is not unfettered, but it must be wide enough for him to assume control of matters concerning internal organization, management and discipline. If he fails to use this discretion properly, he is accountable.

Local financial management (LFM)

Until the Education Act of 1988 came into force governors of LEA maintained schools had very little to do with the financing of their school. Information about the money available to the

school for books and equipment tended to go directly from the LEA to the head, by-passing governors. The costs of keeping the buildings in good order were largely unknown to both the head and the governors: their responsibility has been limited to notifying the LEA that such and such needs doing, only to receive the reply familiar in recent years that 'no money is available'.

The Education Act of 1988 obliged LEAs to delegate to heads and governors every year a far greater degree of control over the budget for their schools. Governors must now* manage the budget and keep accounts, which will be audited by the LEA. Governors can if they wish delegate the management of the budget to the head (in general probably not a good idea since it suggests that the poor devil hasn't already enough to do!) but they retain the overall responsibility. Control of the budget can be taken away from governors and given back to the LEA if governors show themselves to be incompetent.

Each LEA has its own scheme which must be approved by the DES. LEAs are not obliged by law to introduce local financial management into primary schools with fewer than 200 pupils, or into special schools, but can do so if they choose. The whole process is usually called LFM (local financial management) or, in the context of the many post-1988 changes, LMS (local management of schools). The schemes vary somewhat up and down the country and it is vital that all governors know what is in their local scheme and attend the training meetings which LEAs provide. In general the schemes work in the following way.

Each year the LEA determines how much money the school will get, its so-called 'budget share'. The head and governors must then draw up a budget and decide within the budget how much to spend on the items listed below. A typical budget for a primary school and one for a secondary are given in Appendix B.

A very important consideration is that governors can move money from one account to another, a system accountants call 'virement'. You might decide, for example, to put off having classrooms painted for a year in order to put more books into the library.

Staffing

This includes all teaching and non-teaching staff such as

*LEAs have until 1993 to bring in schemes for their areas.

groundsmen, secretarial help, midday supervisors and so on. Governors can decide how many of each to employ.

It should be remembered, of course, that all employees have rights under employment law and you cannot decide willy-nilly to sack a teacher or secretary to buy a new lawnmower! You might, however, decide not to fill a staff vacancy, or delay a replacement, in order to divert funds to some other purpose.

Appointment of staff

Governors of schools with LFM will have to look at their budget and decide how many teaching and non-teaching staff they wish to employ.

When a vacancy arises for a head or deputy the governors must advertise nationally, write to the LEA informing them of the vacancy, receive the applications, draw up a list of those to be interviewed and set up an interviewing panel of at least three governors.

In the case of vacancies for assistant teachers governors must first send a job description of the post to the LEA. They can then decide whether to advertise the post or perhaps offer it to a teacher already at the school. In any case governors must interview any teachers who are nominated by the LEA.

The interviewing of assistant teachers can be done either by one or more governors, the head alone or by a mixture of both. The governing body decides how best to do it.

Governors notify the LEA of whom they have selected. The LEA usually appoint the panel's choice, but once in a while it may turn out that your favourite Dr Smith has an unsavoury past or is otherwise disqualified. This sort of information will be obtained by the LEA when it checks after your meeting. If this happens, you will be asked to go through the appointments procedure again.

The Chief Education Officer for your LEA is entitled to attend all governors' meetings and to offer advice.

Grievances and dismissals

Governors must have agreed procedures for dealing with both of these. Governors can, after seeking the advice of the Chief Education Officer, require the dismissal of a teacher.

Salaries

Teachers' salaries are decided nationally so you have little room to manoeuvre. However, the salary structure allows for so-called 'incentive allowances' and governors have some control over how many of these there are and who receives them. Governors may have some control over wages and salaries paid to other employees. Your clerk will have the details.

Governors also have to pay for 'cover'. Under their contracts of employment (see Appendix A) teachers can be asked to stand in for absent colleagues only for the first day of absence – and not even that if the absence was known about in advance. The head will find someone to fill the gap, but the cost comes from the school budget.

You may have to pay also for 'peripatetic teachers' who visit the school perhaps for half a day or a day each week to teach music, perhaps, or to help children with particular learning difficulties. If individual children are learning to play some musical instrument, however, they can be asked to pay for this.

Examination fees

Governors are often surprised at the total cost of entering pupils for public examinations such as GCSE. This must be paid for out of the budget.

There is a temptation to charge weaker pupils for examination entrance if schools think that their chances of success are slim. This is against the law, however. You can try to get the money back from a pupil who for no good reason simply fails to turn up for the examination and you are entitled to take legal action to recover the debt (if it is worth it!).

Books and equipment

After salaries this may well be the biggest item of expenditure, particularly in secondary schools. You might look around to see where you can buy paper most efficiently and economically, as well as children's exercise books, micro-computers, tape-recorders and so on. It might make sense to go in for consortium buying by working with other schools in the neighbourhood. It might make sense also to shop around for the best deal in photocopiers: should you buy or rent or lease? Obviously the possibilities are enormous.

Running costs of premises

The LEA probably owns your building. This makes the LEA your landlord and you the tenants.

As might be expected, heads and governors must budget for minor repairs such as broken windows or vandalized loos. Major building jobs remain, of course, the responsibility of the landlord. The school playing fields need to be looked after also. Would it be better to employ your own groundsman or get a local firm in to keep things in order? You will almost certainly have to put this out to tender.

School meals

The LEA may run a meals service for you but you may decide to look around for a local catering firm which might offer a better deal. Might it throw in catering at parents' evenings or the school play? It is probably a good idea not to let yourself be carried away by slogans such as 'Say no to privatization!' If your LEA can run school meals better than anyone else it deserves to have the business – but only if.

Under local government law (which applies to governors) there is a general requirement to put contracts 'out to tender', to obtain best value for money. This applies to everything governors do under local financial management. School cleaning is a typical example.

Special educational needs

Governors must bear in mind the extra costs of children with special educational needs when the budget is drawn up.

Pupil support costs

These are to cover items such as uniform, clothing and footwear.

The LEA may well include money for this in your budget and not give permission for 'virement', i.e. they will require you to spend it on welfare and nothing else.

Contingencies

It would be a miracle if something unexpected did not crop up during the year. Perhaps a gathering of your less salubrious 'old pupils' decides to burn down a classroom, or there is a sudden influx of new pupils. Governors will need to budget for unforeseen costs.

Governors will be relieved to know that they are not expected to budget for a share of the costs of running County Hall or the LEA Inspectors, nor for the cost of school buses to bring pupils to school. On the other hand, transport which is necessary as part of the school curriculum — say transport to the local baths or on a short geographical field trip — must be included in the budget.

What if things go wrong?

Governors often express concern about their personal liability if things go wrong when handling such large sums of public money. In a nutshell the legal position is simply that governors are seen as the agents of the LEA in all they do and (gross and extreme cases apart) the LEA carries overall financial responsibility.

Although the introduction of LFM has caused much controversy, it is worth remembering that it amounts to less responsibility than the governors of independent schools have carried literally for centuries.

Curriculum

Governors have always had the authority under the Articles to have a say in the curriculum of their school. In practice, however, they have tended to leave it almost entirely to the head and staff and where governors have attempted to involve themselves more with what is taught they have sometimes met with resentment from teachers. The teaching profession has argued that it is the best judge of what should be taught, a view of course which is unknown in other European countries.

The Education Act of 1988, however, changed things considerably by introducing the National Curriculum, which must be taught in all maintained schools – but not necessarily in independent schools and CTCs. The National Curriculum is described in Chapter 5.

The job of the governors under the new arrangements is to see that the National Curriculum is taught in their school. The wording of the 1988 Act suggests that before the beginning of each school year governors must find out from the LEA what the requirements of the National Curriculum are (remember that these may well change from time to time) and ensure that it will be followed in the school in the coming year.

There are two specific curriculum matters with which governors are also involved:

Sex education. The law requires governors to take 'all reasonable practicable steps' to ensure that any sex education given to pupils is given in such a way as to encourage them to have due regard to moral considerations and the value of family life.

Governors should have a policy on sex education in their school. It would be as well to consider how, for example, homosexuality should be treated.

Schools may not necessarily have a subject on their timetable called 'sex education': it is common for primary teachers in particular to deal with children's questions as they arise. The same is true of many secondary schools. For this reason it may be impracticable for parents to withdraw their children from sex education in the way that they can withdraw them from religious education, because the topic may arise in a health education programme, in biology, in personal, social and moral education issues, in English literature or during tutor group discussions.

This is a very sensitive issue in schools. It could be an item for discussion with parents at the annual governors' meeting. This may be especially important when there is a specific matter, such as teaching about AIDS, to discuss.

Political bias. Schools must by law teach subjects of a political nature in a balanced way, sometimes by presenting opposing cases. An example might be that if the subject of nuclear weapons arises teachers should present the case for 'Peace through NATO' alongside the case for unilateral disarmament, though not necessarily in the same lesson. Governors are required to keep an eye on this in their school – how is not made clear.

Primary school children must not be allowed to take part in

partisan political activities, though they do need to learn what political parties are and what they stand for. Governors must make sure that they deal with any serious examples of political indoctrination, should it occur, rather than panic if an innocent primary child asks about the General Election. Like sex education, this is an area where passions can run high and great tact is needed. Consultation with parents (all of them, not just the enraged few) is essential. The teaching profession has traditionally subscribed overwhelmingly to the view expressed by Parliament. The trouble is that terms such as 'political', 'bias' and 'indoctrination' do not mean the same thing to all those involved.

Admission of pupils

Some LEAs allow their governors to take part in the admission arrangements for pupils to their schools. Governors of voluntary aided schools, CTCs and grant-aided schools have a more direct say in admissions to their schools, so it is worth knowing a little about what the law has to say. Under the principle of 'open enrolment' embodied in the 1988 Education Act, a local education authority cannot impose artificially low entrance quotas on schools simply to balance out numbers in its various schools. It must allow schools to recruit up to their 'standard number', that is the number of pupils they had in 1979 or when they were first opened if they are a new school.

The Education Act of 1980 set out to encourage parents to choose a school carefully for their children and changed the law considerably. The powers of LEAs to send a pupil to any particular school without consultation are much more limited than they used to be. LEAs now must enable parents to say which school they would like their child to attend and must accept this choice, provided that three conditions are met:

(i) that having the pupil at the chosen school does not lead to inefficient education or to 'inefficient use of resources'. It is not clear what this means in practice. Parliamentary law drafters are clever at producing laws which can mean all things to all men and this one is a masterpiece.

(ii) that in the case of aided schools there is no agreement between the governors and the LEA which would be broken if the pupil were to be admitted. Say, for example, that you had an agreement with your LEA that you would always give preference to Anglican pupils for places in your Church of England school. Mr Smith could not insist under the law, therefore, that you took his non-Anglican son.

(iii) that if your school is selective in some way — perhaps a grammar school or a school set up for musicians or ballet dancers — the pupil has also succeeded in whatever entrance tests are normally set.

If parents are unsuccessful in gaining a place at a school for a child, they can turn to an Appeal Panel. These panels were created by the 1980 Act and have been very successful from parents' point of view. The LEA and/or governors *must* tell parents of the existence of the panels and how to apply to them.

They consist of independent experts in education and parents on the one hand, and representatives of the LEA on the other. The key facts are, first, that the LEA nominations may not outnumber the others by more than one and, second, that the chair must not be one of the LEA nominations. This arrangements gives the panels considerable freedom to ignore the views of the LEA or the governors who refused to admit the child in the first place.

The decision of an Appeal Panel is binding on governors, schools and LEAs, but not, oddly enough, on the parents who lose the appeal. They can still take their case to the local government ombudsman if they think that the Appeal Panel has bungled the appeal, but not simply because they disagree with the Panel's decision. In order to go to the ombudsman, incidentally, an offended parent must have the support of one local elected councillor.

Perhaps the greatest effect which Appeal Panels have had is that LEA, governors and headteachers must now define very closely just what they mean by the bland statement 'the school is full'. At one time it was virtually impossible for a parent to challenge the statement. Nowadays an Appeal Panel will probe very carefully indeed. Are you sure that you couldn't get just one more child into Mrs Smith's third year junior class? And if it happens that Wayne's fourth year subject choices would put him in to the smallest groups, could he not be admitted?

A very important fact is that, as the law stands, an Appeal Panel can allow pupils into your school above any admission limit set by you or the LEA, subject of course to the three limitations outlined above.

School discipline

Discipline is part of the day-to-day running of the school, of course, and as such comes largely under the head's duty of 'internal management', as mentioned above.

"ITEM SIX ... SCHOOL DISCIPLINE ..."

Governors have a major part to play when things go badly wrong and a pupil is excluded from school by the head. The head must inform the governors who can, if they wish, overrule the head and reinstate the pupil. The governors must also hear any appeal by the parents of an excluded pupil. Incidentally, the terms 'suspension' and 'expulsion' are no longer used officially: what used to be called 'expulsion' is now referred to as 'permanent exclusion'.

A pupil who is under 18 cannot appeal by himself or herself; it is the parents who have the right of appeal. It is sad to think that so often pupils who are excluded come from very unsatisfactory homes where the parents probably couldn't care less whether their child is excluded or not and can't be bothered to appeal. In such cases a wrongful exclusion only adds to the pupil's problems and sense of injustice.

If governors decide that the head has made the correct decision and that the pupil should remain excluded from school, or if it looks as if the pupil is likely to miss more than five days school in any term because of exclusion, the LEA must be informed without delay. Parliament has decided also that governors and the LEA must be informed if a pupil is likely to miss any public examination because of exclusion.

When a LEA has been told of an exclusion it has to go through the matter again and itself listen to another appeal by the parents. The LEA can order the governors and the head to readmit the pupil. The matter doesn't necessarily end there, however. The governors are entitled to appeal to the LEA against the LEA order to readmit. It could, as they used to say on *Monty Python*, get very silly.

Governors of aided and special agreement schools are in a slightly different position and should check with the clerk to the governors.

Governors also have a part to play in setting up the disciplinary policy for their school. Governors can give the head their views on school discipline and the head must have regard to them. Generally speaking the standard of behaviour in the school is still determined by the head so far as it is not laid down by the governors. A statement of disciplinary policy by governors to the head must, however, be in writing.

Just in case your governing body is dominated by hangers and floggers, remember that corporal punishment was made illegal by the Education Act of 1986. The ban extends to all pupils who receive public funds for their education, such as subsidized pupils at independent schools. It does not yet apply to other pupils at independent schools, although it is probably only a matter of time before it does.

'In pursuance of the statutory obligation to parents under Section 30 of the Education (no 2) Act 1986, this report describes the discharge by the Governing Body of their functions in relation to the school.'

The sentence above, it was decided by one LEA in 1987, should be the words with which all its governors began their annual report to parents. An annual meeting at which governors meet parents to discuss their report on the school is not in itself a bad idea, but the event could be killed stone dead if the approach is entirely bureaucratic. The 1986 Act does indeed require governors to produce a report, but not to cure all local insomniacs.

The law says nothing about the way in which a report to parents should be written beyond saying that it should be 'brief as is reasonably consistent with . . . its contents'. There is everything to be gained by making it simple, friendly and free from professional jargon. The purpose of the report is to inform parents about what you have been doing for the school since the last annual meeting and to say what you think lies ahead. The meeting to discuss the report provides an opportunity to ask for views on any issues you may be thinking about and generally also to listen. Governors are not meant to be on trial, although during the first round of annual meetings in 1987 there were a few red faces when parents asked 'How many governors' meetings did Mr X attend last year?' On the other hand it is very useful indeed to governors to have a storm of protest about the state of the school's physics laboratory, the shortage of books or equipment, or the quality of teaching, so that they can see that something is actually done about it.

The information about the school which the law requires you to give is:

* To say *when and where* the annual parents' meeting is to take place.

* To say that there will be a *discussion* of what you and they wish to raise. In this connection it may be worthwhile to point out that the chairman will not permit the meeting to be used as an opportunity for Mrs Murgatroyd to have a personal go at the head, or any member of staff. Something

in the report like 'Parents are asked to remember that if they have some *personal problem* to do with the school they should tell the chairman of governors or the headteacher. Discussions of a personal nature will probably not be of interest to other parents and would only delay the annual meeting', would probably do the trick.

* To say what you have done about any *resolutions* passed at last year's annual meeting with parents. Governors have to 'consider' any resolutions passed at such a meeting, but this does not mean that they must simply do as they are told. There may be very good reasons why all the third forms cannot study basket-weaving or visit the local coalmine, despite what the parents resolved. In any case, if there were only 220 parents there out of a possible 1000 you are entitled to think that that is not sufficient to justify major upheavals at your school. However, you do have to tell the parents why you have not acted on their resolutions – and perhaps be sent back to think again.

* To give the *names of all the governors* and where they come from – that is, whether they are parent governors, co-opted, or whatever. The addresses of the chairman and the clerk must be given. The addresses of other governors are not needed for the report, but it is a good idea perhaps to put in a phone number or two (with the permission of the people concerned) where governors can be reached if necessary. Parents must also be told when the term of office of each governor expires (with elections in mind!).

* To explain the arrangements as far as possible for the *next election of parent governors.*

* To give parents a statement of the *running costs* of the school for the year and how you as governors have spent any school funds at your disposal. At the moment the LEA has to provide this for the governors but in future it is likely that governors will be able to provide their own (see pp. 27–32).

* To give summaries of the results obtained by your pupils in any *public examinations* such as GCSE and A level, or the national tests for all children at the ages of 7, 11 and 14, introduced by the 1988 Education Act, 'though the individual scores of 7-year-olds may not be made public'.

39

* To describe the *curriculum* of the school. A chart is probably the best way of doing this.

* To say how the school is developing *links with the community*. You are supposed also to say what links you have with the police (you may not be terribly proud of some of these!).

* To produce the report in *languages other than English* if you think it worthwhile. In principle this is an excellent idea for community relations, but it can cause problems if, like some schools in London, the pupils of your school speak thirty-odd languages between them. Some commonsense is needed here. There is no obligation to produce a translation into Turkish for one family, for example.

The report must be sent to the parents of all children at the school at least two weeks before the meeting, and a copy must be kept at the school for anyone to see at all reasonable times. The best way is probably to keep a copy with the minutes of regular meetings on the governors' notice board near the school entrance.

It is not a good idea to have the headteacher write the governors' report and it was disappointing during the first round of parents' meetings in 1987 to see how many clearly had been written entirely by the head. The Education Act intended the report to be from the governors to parents. Obviously a lot of information in the report has to come from the head, and it is fully in order to ask for it, but the writing should be done by the governors, probably not even by the clerk. If the head has chosen to be a governor, presumably s/he can be persuaded in an armlock by the others to write it, but that only serves to reinforce the notion which is all too often in parents' minds that you as governors simply do what you are told to do by the head and can't even write a report of your own . . . If the headteacher is not a governor it is doubtful in law whether s/he can be required by you to produce the report – only notes of information to go into it.

Minutes and proceedings

The minutes of all governors' meetings, draft and signed, as well as all reports, documents and papers discussed by the governors have to be available at the school 'to persons wishing to inspect them'. It is probably a good idea to pin them on the governors'

40

notice board in the school, and it is very much against the spirit
of the rules to keep them locked up in the head's filing cabinet, to
be fished out only on request.

Governors' meetings

The Education (School Government) Regulations of 1987 have a
lot to say about this.

Meetings must be held at least once each school term. The clerk
to the governors actually calls meetings but must follow any dates
set by the previous meeting or by the chair in his official capacity.

Any three governors can ask for a meeting at any time, and the
clerk to the governors must call one if they do.

The quorum for termly governors' meetings is one third of the
members, rounded up to a whole number. LEA can put a bigger
quorum into the Articles of Government for their school if they
wish, but it must not be larger than two fifths. If the *annual
parents' meeting* wishes to pass formal resolutions, the number of
parents present must equal 20 per cent of the number of pupils in
the school.

There is an important exception, however. If the governors'
meeting wants to co-opt other governors, the quorum goes up to
three quarters, again rounded up to a whole number. This again
emphasizes the particular need for all governors to turn up for the
first meeting of the year. The three quarters quorum also applies
in the very special case where governors of a maintained boarding
school meet to appoint a parent governor: elections in such a case
would be difficult because by and large the parents of children in
a boarding school know each other less well.

Annual parents' meeting. Once a year, as described above,
governors must hold a meeting with the parents (and guardians)
of children at the school. At the meeting they must discuss the
affairs of the school as described in the annual governors' report
(see pp. 38–40).

Withdrawal from meetings. As is general in local and national
government, governors who are likely to profit financially from
anything being discussed at meetings should leave the room
while that item is being discussed. They certainly should not take
part in the discussion or cast a vote on it. This applies also to a
governor's husband or wife and any relatives living with them.

The principle of being an interested party goes further and is

41

largely a matter of commonsense. If your spouse with whom you are living is up for a job at the school or liable to be transferred, sacked or promoted, or your own child is up before the governors for some disciplinary offence, then obviously you cannot take part in that meeting – nor can you if the question arises of whether to admit a child of your own to the school. You must also leave (even if you are the clerk) if the subject under discussion is some possible disciplinary action against you.

In the interests of impartial justice it follows also that you cannot be a member of an appeal panel involving some action which you yourself started. For example, if you see Wayne, Shane and Duane creating mayhem behind the bikeshed, report them to the head and the head takes disciplinary action before the governors, you must withdraw from that meeting – although the governors of course may call you as a witness. In such cases the head, too, can only be a witness and not a governor. The point is that the governors must be seen to be unbiassed in the case.

The list of reasons for withdrawal given above and in the DES Regulations is not necessarily complete. As the result of a legal action by a teacher in 1986, it is now the case that LEA may add other reasons for withdrawal to the list, probably by putting them into your Articles of Government. For example, it is now common to exclude teacher governors from meetings if what is being discussed is the appointment or promotion of a teacher who is senior to the teacher governor.

Whom do you represent at meetings?

Obviously you will feel a degree of loyalty to the group which asked the LEA to put you there.

However, once you are made a governor you are a member in your own right and not a delegate. This means that you are free to vote exactly as you think fit as an individual charged with the best interests of your school, even if on occasion this might run counter to the group which put you there. In practice this issue arises most frequently in the case of parent governors, particularly where you may have to represent as many as 2,000 parents in a big comprehensive school. Parent governors can find themselves pressurized by articulate groups of parents with a particular view of what should happen; or even be lobbied by two opposing camps. The task of the parent governor is to speak up for parents as a group, not for only a few of them.

Finally, if ever you are obliged not to support your own group's views at governors' meetings, do not let threats of being 'unseated' tempt you to break the rules about confidentiality, or you risk alienating your group, your fellow governors and the LEA.

Confidentiality

A word of warning. Governors are in a privileged position and will often come into possession of information which, in the interests of all, should remain confidential. You may be called upon, for example, to decide what is to be done about the continuing education of a girl who has just given birth at fourteen to an illegitimate child. To talk about the case around your community would be a grave breach of the trust invested in you.

Although commonsense suggests that some matters, as for example the above, ought to be regarded as confidential, it should be borne in mind that *everything* is in fact confidential. There are very good reasons for this. One is that governors would be less likely to speak their mind if they thought that everything they said was going to be reported elsewhere, perhaps in the local press. Sometimes, too, a decision taken by the governors is later shown to be inappropriate when additional information comes to light and obliges them to change their mind. Beware, too, of publicly discussing allegations which may be made at a meeting; quite often they turn out to have been false.

Because of this confidentiality, you are given by law what is called 'qualified privilege'. Like MPs when they are in the Commons you can say exactly what you like without the fear of legal action being taken against you. But this privilege covers you only during formal governors' meetings and not outside; nor are you at all protected if it can be shown that you spoke in malice, and you must watch what you say if your meeting is held in public.

You may perhaps feel that the system is set up in order to gag you; this is a false impression. The minutes of governors' meetings must be published and made available at your school for anyone who may wish to see them. This is an excellent way of keeping in touch with your community, but it should be the only formal way. Unofficial breaches of confidentiality are likely to make you very unpopular with your fellow governors and might lead to your dismissal from the governing body.

Other duties not laid down by law

There are some other things that governing bodies frequently have to do which are not prescribed by law.

(1) *Consult and listen to the views of the teaching and non-teaching staffs of the school.* Usually this takes place through the headteacher or representatives, but it is a good idea to have an occasional get-together (preferably informal, perhaps over tea and cakes in the Domestic Science block). This is a good way for any governor to get the 'feel' of a school, and meet both teaching and non-teaching staff.

(2) *Decide on means of consulting parents and the local community about matters affecting the school.* To some extent this will happen already if your school has a parent-teacher association, but do not forget that many parents who could have useful things to say may not be members of the PTA. Even if all parents are technically members of the PTA, many might prefer to talk to a governor, especially a parent governor, in confidence. Not everyone has the courage to stand up and make a point at your annual meeting with parents.

(3) *Discuss any reports about the school, either by the headteacher or the local education authority.* Occasionally the school may undergo an inspection by Her Majesty's Inspectors of Schools (HMIs) or LEA Inspectors. The governors should be asked for their views while the Inspectors are preparing their report, and the final version should be discussed at a governors' meeting.

The headteacher usually prepares a report for each governors' meeting as a matter of course, but it is quite in order for you to ask in advance for information to be included on matters which interest the governors particularly, and which otherwise might not come up. Nor is there any reason why you should not ask for special reports from time to time, provided these concern topics of genuine concern and importance, and are not just a means of satisfying your personal curiosity. Preparing a report takes valuable time from the head and teachers which might be better spent working with children.

44

If you are discussing matters connected with the curriculum or general conduct of the school, you may well feel the need of outside advice, in addition to that offered by the headteacher. One person to approach here is the Chief Adviser or Inspector to your local education authority. He works in the education department and may well be prepared to come to one of your meetings. In certain circumstances also, your local HMI may be willing to help, and his office can usually be found in the local telephone directory under Department of Education and Science.

You may well also be asked to prepare reports yourself. The local education authority might ask to know what you propose to do about, for example, vandalism of the school buildings both during and outside school hours. Usually it is the clerk to the governors who actually writes the report after the discussion at the governors' meeting.

Your local authority will also expect its governors to keep it informed about the current state of the school buildings and furniture, which, incidentally, includes any decoration which becomes necessary, and the quality of the heating, lighting and sanitary arrangements. When you hear that large-scale building is taking place near your school, it will be up to you to ensure that the local authority is both aware of what is happening and is planning the extra school places necessary.

(4) It may be possible for you as governors to control the *letting of the school building when it is not in use for normal school activities*. This is a good opportunity to encourage links with the community and various social groups — and it might be possible to divert some of the proceeds from the lettings into the school funds.

(5) From time to time you will need to check that the arrangements for dealing with *fire at school* are satisfactory. It is common practice for schools to have firedrills, and you should check that these are recorded in the headteacher's report to the governors. The head will usually tell you of any problems here, and how long it takes to get all the pupils out of the building.

(6) Occasionally you will be called upon to decide on grievances which are put to you. As employees, assistant teachers and heads have a *procedure for settling grievances* which is part of their conditions of service. Briefly, when a dispute is formally notified to you in writing, you must hold a meeting within ten days, and invite the people involved to attend. You must come to a decision on the basis of what they tell you, and any reports or other documents you receive.

(7) You may from time to time receive reports about the way the system of *school dinners* is operating. Your school will in all probability have a separate staff to cook and serve the meals: there will be a cook supervisor in charge. In many schools the head takes care of the dining arrangements but in very large schools it may be the case that the system is administered directly from County Hall and the head has little to do with it.

Your job as a governor is to see that all is well with the system, and particularly to ensure that the premises are adequate. If they are not, you should press the LEA until they are. There are detailed building regulations which specify how much room is to be used for school meals. The clerk will have information on this.

At present only needy pupils whose parents receive Income Support will be automatically entitled to school meals or refreshment; other children may have school meals if your LEA chooses to provide them. This is a considerable change from the former position whereby all children were entitled to meals. Furthermore, your LEA will have to provide facilities for pupils who bring sandwiches or other refreshment to school for lunch.

In the last few years difficulties have arisen over the supervision of pupils at lunchtime. At one time these duties were carried out by the teaching staff of the school and there was a general assumption by all that this was a normal part of teachers' duties. Nowadays such duties are voluntary, a free meal usually being provided for the teachers on duty.

Opinion in the teaching profession is divided. Many teachers take the view that a break at lunchtime is their right: in practice the free time is often taken up anyway in preparing for the afternoon session. Others take the more extreme view that the social need for the whole school meals service has now disappeared, since malnutrition among children is largely a thing of the past. They object to being treated as child-minders while mothers are relieved of a cooking burden at lunchtime, or go out to work. Others are prepared to see the school lunch as part of the social life of the school, a chance for the pupils to meet children other than their classmates.

Since these duties are now voluntary, despite the fact that many teachers do still volunteer, LEAs employ so-called 'supervisors' to look after the children at lunchtime.

(8) You will from time to time have to consider the matter of *staff absences*. The LEA will usually have clear policies about

whether their teachers may have time off with pay in order to attend conferences or deal with urgent domestic matters and so on. It often happens that teachers are absent for reasons which are outside the policy as laid down, but which might seem to you nevertheless to be very good ones. In such cases you would pass a resolution at the meeting that the teacher should be paid. There is no obligation on you to do so, however, and you must judge each case on its merits.

Being a governor of a non-maintained school

These schools are usually referred to as 'independent', because they are almost entirely responsible for their own affairs, and are largely independent of both the DES and LEA. For this reason the governing body and the head carry considerably more responsibility for the success of the school than is the case in state schools.

Much time is spent at governors' meetings in discussing finance, and the governing body will include people highly skilled in such matters. It is up to you and colleagues to find the money to pay for the running of the school on a day-to-day basis, and to finance new developments and keep the school up to date. Buildings are inevitably perhaps the greatest problem, since they are by now probably fairly old and in need of constant maintenance.

Independent schools find their money through fees paid for pupils, through investments of all sorts, and frequently through appeals to the community and former students for specific projects such as science buildings or sports facilities.

All independent schools are required to be registered with the DES; and there is a Registrar of Independent Schools. This system is designed to ensure that the school reaches a minimum standard of efficiency. After inspection by HMI many schools are officially regarded as efficient. In extreme cases it is possible for the DES to declare a person to be unfit to teach in an independent school, or to be the proprietor of one. Here again, the DES word is law, although there is of course a machinery for appeals.

Governors of independent boarding schools tend to be less directly involved with parents and the local community than their counterparts in state schools, because inevitably their pupils come from far away, even overseas. This is not true, of course, of public day schools, which have distinctly local connections and are run very much in the grammar school tradition.

Unless governors take considerable care, there is a real danger that the very worthwhile and valuable independence enjoyed by their school might cut them off from possibly beneficial outside influences, which at worst could lead to an undesirable educational isolation. Whereas LEAs run professional courses for their teachers, for example, provision for teachers in independent schools is limited to the relatively few courses run nationally by DES and universities. Similarly the services of LEA advisers are not normally available, although in this respect use can and indeed should be made of local HMI.

Relationships between independent schools and LEA are generally good and it is worthwhile to foster them at all levels. Indeed, one justification of the independent sector in British education is that it can bring more people into decision-making in education if it works well.

Relations with the local authority

As you emerge, perhaps very confused, from your first meeting you will probably remember hearing people say: 'I wonder if County Hall will agree to that?' or 'Perhaps we ought to ask the Director'. Probably, too, there will have been general grumbles about the all-important 'Works Department', which hasn't sent anyone, despite all your requests, to repair the window in Classroom 3.

In Great Britain education is part of the machinery of local government: your local county council has an education sub-committee just as it has a housing sub-committee, a finance sub-committee and many others. In day-to-day usage teachers and officials tend to refer simply to the 'Education Committee', but in fact the education committee, like the others, is responsible to the full county council, and in the last resort may be overruled by that council, though in practice this rarely happens except over contentious issues.

The Education Committee appoints a Chief Education Officer – some authorities use instead the older title, Director of Education – to manage the system in the area. The job is a very difficult and complex one, and not easy to define. He or she is not the slave of the committee and required to do no more than carry out policy decisions. Parliament has decreed that each local authority shall have a Chief Education Officer, even if it thinks it can manage without one. Moreover, the DES takes a close interest in who is appointed to the job, as was shown when the Inner London Education Authority was disbanded and the boroughs appointed new chief officers.

The Chief Education Officer provides the top leadership in a system containing hundreds of schools. Education is the largest of the social services, and in your area may well be spending at the moment well over one million pounds every week. On the one hand the Chief Education Officer will work within LEA policy, and from time to time generate considerable steam if that policy is not carried out further down the line. On the other he has great influence on the shaping of policy through attendance at meetings of the Education Committee and his relationship to the chairman, with whom he works closely. Together they must ensure that the resources necessary to keep the system running are available. Yet formidable as this team might seem to be, they are far from being dictators, whether they wish to be or not. The Chief Education Officer has to keep abreast with the almost daily flood of administrative memoranda, circulars and statutory instruments from the DES which land on his desk, not to mention sizeable, possibly acrimonious correspondence with heads, governors, teachers' unions or parents. For their part, politicians have to keep an eye on the wishes of their electors and interested pressure groups, of whom of course governors should rightly be one.

There is never enough money available for education, and it is probably fair to say that most Chief Education Officers and their committees in recent times have been less concerned with progress and pushing forward into new fields than making the available resources stretch thinly to cover areas of desperate need. Much time is inevitably spent on deciding priorities, and this is where you as a governor have a role to play. Should your very popular and overcrowded school have an extension built, or should someone else's school, twenty miles away, still working in a building put up in 1862, be completely replaced? Should the buildings to complete the plan for a local comprehensive school be started next year, or should the money be used to get rid of all the outside toilets which freeze up in winter, many of which are a health hazard?

There is no simple answer to any of these problems, and none that will please everybody. It is up to you and your fellow governors to bring whatever pressure you can to bear. Imagine that there is, up at County Hall, a long list of jobs waiting to be done: where your job appears on the list may well be up to you. Remember, too, that even if a list of priorities has been agreed, it will be reviewed at fairly frequent intervals. Find out when it is to be reviewed, and if your efforts meet with no luck now, you may well get somewhere in a few months.

The job of the Chief Education Officer and his staff could thus be described as getting the best educational value for money, and encouraging and supporting the best practices in schools and teaching.

County Hall staff

If in the course of your duties you have to visit County Hall for the first time you are likely to find the experience traumatic. As you wander the long anonymous corridors past the peeling splendour of the Alderman Harry Ramsbottom Committee Room, clutching your petition, compass and thermos flask, you half expect to turn a corner and trip over the dusty skeletons of some other ill-fated governors' expedition which never quite

made it to U.R. Smith-Jones of Buildings and Special Projects, not, of course, to be confused with R.U. Smith-Jones of Staffing and Salaries.

In practice, most of your dealings with County Hall will be by letter from your clerk to the appropriate office. If, for example, an item appears on the agenda for one of your meetings about whether Mr Boreham of the French Department at your school should be paid for a day when he was absent, your clerk will know who can pronounce on official policy. On the other hand, it is certainly worthwhile to know how the Education Department at County Hall works, and there may well be instances when you would like to talk face to face with the official concerned: this could happen perhaps on site when additional buildings are being discussed.

It is easiest to think of the education staff at County Hall as falling into two separate groups, the professional team of advisers, and the administrators, both of which are directly responsible to the Chief Education Officer. In New York it has been decided that educational administrators should live where the action is, so that they are mostly to be found in various schools rather than in a central palace.

The inspection and advisory service

Just as managers of industry need to keep themselves and the workforce in touch with new developments in order to survive economically, so it is obviously in the interests of the education service for the LEA as employers to endeavour to keep the service up to date.

Most LEAs now appoint Advisers who are concerned with what is taught in schools and how. In the case of primary schools, Advisers are usually interested in the work of the school as a whole, for secondary and middle schools there are Advisers in individual subjects such as Maths, Physical Education or Modern Languages. Generally speaking they work as a team under the leadership of the Chief Adviser.

As their title suggests, it is the job of Advisers to advise, though increasingly they are now called Inspectors and are given a more investigative role. They advise the Chief Education Officer of new developments, and through him or her of course, the Education Committee itself. If, for example, schools are turning to new Science courses in the sixth form, then the Committee will be faced with additional expenditure on new and expensive equipment. Perhaps social problems in inner city schools suggest strongly that resources should be diverted from other areas to the schools there.

Advisers should be in and out of your school fairly regularly, talking to heads and teachers about new ideas and developments. Often they hold so-called 'in-service' courses, perhaps on your school premises, at which teachers gather to talk about what they are doing. Because they know the schools and the teachers in their area well, they are often useful members of appointment committees, and can tell you as governors which of the people who have applied to be in charge of music at your school are likely to be good value. If a young teacher has arrived at your school straight from college or university and is having difficulties, it is likely that the appropriate Adviser will soon be involved.

Advisers are sensitive about their relationships with schools, and they usually make it clear to teachers that their advice does not have to be acted upon but should be at least seriously considered. Teachers often find their help extremely valuable, though there are sometimes grumbles that they do not spend enough time in schools, which is partly explained by the many other commit-ments they have to undertake.

The administrative staff

It is not possible to generalize about exactly who works for whom at County Hall, since each Chief Education Officer will have personal ideas about the best way to organize his staff. The senior staff below the CEO and his deputy usually carry the rank and title of Assistant Director or Assistant Education Officer and one of them will usually be at the head of each section. It will be worth your while to find out the names of your section heads. The sections are usually:

Further education, dealing with courses for pupils beyond the age of sixteen. Not only the colleges of further education are involved here, but also technical colleges and in some areas sixth form or tertiary colleges. Adult education figures here also. Apart from administering the institutions themselves, this section is responsible for the payment of grants to eligible students to cover tuition fees, maintenance and so on.

The universities are national rather than local institutions, since in general their students come from a wide area of the country. Polytechnics are no longer administered from County Hall, but there may well be a section there with the title *Higher Education* to which queries about, for example, grants to undergraduate students may be made.

Schools. This section will be divided up into primary and secondary divisions. There will also probably be a division which looks after special schools, for children with learning difficulties or emotional disturbances, and for those who are officially recognized as educationally sub-normal.

The work here is concerned with the staffing of schools, deciding how many teachers a school should have, and paying teachers' salaries. It will deal with queries about the allocation of pupils to schools, and general matters in the day-to-day running of schools.

Common Services. This is usually a big section dealing with all those services one can too easily take for granted in the running of schools. Its responsibilities include looking after playing fields and supplies of all sorts to schools, from books to equipment. It looks after the maintenance of schools, school caretakers, and administers the School Meals Service. It also has a host of smaller responsibilities such as the provision of school transport where needed, road safety and so on.

Development. In addition to looking after existing schools, local authorities must also have an eye to the future. Housing estates, even new towns, spring up and require new schools or extensions to existing ones. It takes years to get a school from the point at which the decision is made to build to the moment when the first pupils arrive, and, since pupils have a statutory right to a school place, local education authorities cannot afford to be caught out. For the same reason, they have to keep well informed about movements in the child population, which of course, may not go hand in hand with new housing. At the same time, fashions in education change, and local authorities need to gaze into the crystal ball to ensure that the schools they build now will serve the needs of the future. Will schools in twenty years' time be generally the same size as they are now? Will they still have classrooms as we know them? Will there be more learning from machines? Above all, will the schools be in the right places? And is the right place in a town centre or in the green belt? The Development Section copes daily with these nightmares.

The Area Education Officer

The original local authorities for education one hundred years ago were countless so-called School Boards, some tiny, some, such as London, obviously very much bigger. In general though they had very much a grassroots local flavour. In 1902 they were largely taken over by the then new local authorities based on counties and county boroughs, and education became, as it is now, part of the machinery of local government. Since that time political and economic changes have reduced the number of local education authorities to the small total of authorities we have today.

The bigger local authorities have grown, so they have had to take care not to get out of touch with what is happening at the community or local level. For this reason they usually set up Area Education Offices locally, headed by the Area Education Officer. Their principal function is to act as the eyes and ears of County Hall and to liaise between it and schools.

Beyond that the actual duties of the Area Education Officer vary between local authorities: almost certainly he or his deputy will be acting as the clerk to your governing body, and will thus handle most of your correspondence. He will also be involved in making staff appointments at your school, particularly the senior ones, and his office will be in almost daily contact with the head and school secretary over a whole host of routine matters. He is your best source of information about what is happening in your area in the field of education.

Her Majesty's Inspectors of Schools

HMIs, as they are usually called, should not be confused with the local authority Advisers we referred to earlier, although in many ways their functions are similar. The essential and traditional difference is that they are an almost entirely independent body and give the help and advice they think is called for in any given situation, and are not necessarily bound by the dictates of local authority policy. Indeed it is one of their strengths that they can, and do from time to time, criticize local education authorities and the way their schools are working.

The title 'Inspector' is slightly misleading nowadays. Until fairly recently teams of HMIs used to visit schools at intervals, and as many as ten or twelve in some cases would spend a week or more sitting in classes, talking to heads and staff and generally shining bright torches into dark corners. Afterwards they would prepare a full report on what they had seen, and submit it, without fear or favour, to schools, governors and LEA for their action. There was no power to order anyone to carry out their recommendations, but the influence of these reports was nevertheless enormous on everyone. The language in which they were traditionally written was often the source of some amusement. Rarely, if ever, did they say 'Mr Jones is a fool': instead they would say 'The red-haired man with one ear and leg who teaches Latin to Form 2 is . . .', and consequently the game of 'Guess who that is' was very popular in staff rooms when reports appeared.

Full inspections still occur as do shorter flying visits known as 'dipsticks'. One of your most important duties as governor occurs if you meet the reporting HMI following an official inspection of your school.

HMIs keep in touch with schools through the courses they run for teachers, and you will hear, at meetings, of teachers asking for time off during term to attend them. Such courses are usually very popular indeed, since HMIs know what is going on in the country as a whole, far beyond the limits of your county area, and this is reflected in their courses. Although you may not actually see much of them, they are very influential behind the scenes, particularly in dealings between local education authorities and the DES in London. They are sometimes called in whenever, sadly, a crisis point is reached somewhere.

HMIs are led by a Senior Chief Inspector of schools and have their headquarters at the DES in London. They have local offices also and there will almost certainly be one or more HMI there with a brief to watch over your school. The local offices are not at County Hall, but as mentioned earlier, can be found in the telephone book under Department of Education and Science.

Visiting County Hall

Your link with the thinking at County Hall is the clerk to your governing body, and he or she will see to it that matters of concern automatically appear on the agenda for your meetings. However, there is something to be said for keeping yourself, as a governor, well informed directly. You can do this by attending meetings of the Education Committee of your local authority.

One advantage of doing this is that you will get advance warning of what is happening in the area, and to some extent this will combat the feeling that governors sometimes have that everything has been finally decided before they even hear about it. This does not mean that local authorities are deliberately secretive about what they do. Since education com-mittees have to have their decisions approved by the full County Council before they are implemented, the Chief Education Officer cannot act until he has that approval. He may not act in a hurry, therefore, in case that approval is not given.

You can obtain details of Education Committee and County Council meetings either from your clerk, or from County Hall directly. By Act of Parliament (the Public Bodies (Admission to Meetings) Act, 1960) the public must be admitted to meetings. It is a sad fact of life, though, that not many members of the public take up their rights in this respect.

Sometimes these meetings are held without the press or public being admitted, but it must be stressed that this is the exception rather than the rule. Indeed Parliament has made it deliberately more difficult to do that. The committee has to pass a formal resolution to go into secret session, and must give the reason in the text of the resolution. This means that it is possible afterwards to see if the committee had good reason for its actions. Incidentally, such a resolution has to cover only specific items on the agenda, and cannot be used to exclude the public from a whole meeting.

This has probably been the most formidable chapter of the book for you to read. If you are still masochistic enough to continue as a governor, and we recommend strongly that you do, despite the, on the surface, intimidating responsibilities, then we shall move on to consider in more detail how you can try to do this immensely worthwhile job well, or, if you are a seasoned old lag, even better.

3

Being an effective
school governor

If a governing body is to be effective then a group of individuals, some of whom may never have met before, must become a team and set out to work for the good of the school and its community. This implies keeping up to date about what is going on in education generally and in the school in particular, and pooling the talents and knowledge of politicians, parents, teachers and others in the locality to facilitate the successful running of the school. In this chapter we consider the roles of various kinds of governor, how governors can be trained, and what they can do to help schools.

Political nominees

The governor chosen by a political party to serve as a local education authority nominee can be in a difficult position. Most people directly involved in schools – parents, teachers, pupils – do not see education in political terms at all. Although this can be said to be a naive view of life, it describes the vantage point of a sizeable chunk of humanity. Whether political party X or election manifesto Y is for or against some educational proposal is largely irrelevant unless it affects their own school. The tendency in some areas to nominate political governors entirely from one party is greatly resented by many people.

Consequently political nominees may be viewed with some suspicion by other governors for several reasons. They may be seen as 'professional' governors, serving on several schools' governing bodies whilst not especially committed to any one of them, whereas parent or teacher governors see themselves as concerned only with the one school. They may be regarded as outsiders, perhaps not even living in the area and therefore not knowledgeable about local problems. Worst of all they may be perceived as 'lobby fodder', blindly following the national or local party political line on issues irrespective of the arguments surrounding them.

Political nominees are thus in a similar position to the Member of Parliament, elected by perhaps less than half their constituents, yet duty bound to represent all of them whether they voted for them or not. They face exactly the same kinds of dilemma. A Member of Parliament may find himself voting against his party after some important debate because his own constituents might suffer if the proposed measure became law. A governor may discover that his party's line on an educational issue is in sharp conflict with what his judgement tells him to be appropriate for his particular school.

The strength, on the other hand, of the politically nominated governor can be that he has often accrued great experience of local government, understands the workings of County Hall, and may be a member of some of its key committees, has served on other governing bodies, may have considerable local, regional and national knowledge on certain issues, and has been democratically elected to serve the people, albeit sometimes after a low poll. There is no universally agreed blueprint for success, but the following pieces of advice may be helpful to politically nominated governors.

DO   – Use your knowledge of local government to help your fellow governors. If you are also a member of other local government committees, help your school there as well.

            – Try to treat each school as special, even if you belong to more than one governing body. Empathize with parents and teachers who are totally committed to 'their' school.

- Attend regularly, not just when something controversial is under discussion.
- Admit you are not too familiar with some issues
under consideration, even if you have been on the
education committee for years. Councillors who feign
great wisdom about everything are rapidly rumbled,
those who are willing to learn, no matter how
experienced, are greatly respected.

DON'T   — Blind your fellow governors with procedural wizardry.
Most are amateurs at committee work and do not like
to feel humiliated if they speak out of turn or do not
understand committee ways.
- Toe the party line blindly. Think about each move. If
you were elected on a 'save money' ticket, remember
that education does cost money, and help to avoid
waste rather than squash every initiative. Don't jump
to conclusions about what 'waste' is. Find out!
- Fight the governors higher up. It is two-faced to be
silent at a governors' meeting and then oppose their
proposal at the education committee or elsewhere.
Speak your mind at the governors' meeting, then if
you argue against the issue subsequently people will
respect your openness.
- Over-play the caucus by always voting as a block
because you and your colleagues have decided to stick
together on every issue on a 'LEA versus the rest'
principle.
- Constantly compare the school unfavourably with
others you know. It is unfair when few people present
can verify or refute your statements. There is a
diplomatic way of letting fellow governors know
what other schools of your acquaintance do in similar
circumstances to the ones under discussion.

Parents

Parent governors have been elected by the body of parents, many
of whom may not know their nominee even by sight. It is quite a
good idea for parent governors to give some thought to this
problem. For example, there is no reason why parent governors
should not be introduced at meetings of the parent teacher

association, if there is one, or at a parents' evening. It simply requires the person running the meeting to ask the parent governors to stand up and be seen. We are all used to seeing a couple of self-conscious beetroot faces surface briefly and then subside amid good-natured and curious banter. 'So that's him, then. Don't like his tie' is just one of the hazards of being, however modestly, in public life.

"....AND I KNOW THE HEADMASTER WILL JOIN ME IN CONGRATULATING MR. BASHER ON BEING ELECTED PARENT GOVERNOR"

Similarly a recent photograph and the name of each parent governor can be put on a poster and displayed prominently when there is a meeting of parents. There is no point in having parent governors and then not knowing who they are.

Representing the parents' point of view when any school's parents may represent all conceivable views under the sun on any issue is not straightforward. It is helpful, therefore, if parent governors try to get around their 'parish' making sure they listen sympathetically to opinions which conflict with their own. Parent governors who speak only for themselves or for the benefit of their own children become notorious. A parent arguing strongly for favourable treatment of one group may, by implication, be arguing for less favourable treatment of another. For example, if the parent of a keen gymnast pressed for classes of four in gymnastics, the parents of dance enthusiasts might find their children in a class of forty.

One way of communicating with parents is to ask the governors to agree to the school distributing a newsletter to all parents whenever they send out a mailing. Schools often send letters home about plays, concerts, open days or parents' evenings and one extra paper can easily be added. It can be translated into other languages if the school serves a multiracial community. A brief chatty letter might read something like this:

Dear Parent

You may be interested to know one or two things which have been happening at governors' meetings recently. At our March meeting the headmaster explained about the national tests for 7- and 11-year-olds. There will be a meeting for all parents early next term to discuss this.

One of us was part of a deputation to County Hall earlier this month to see if we could get the building of the changing room accommodation at Top Field speeded up. We were assured that this would be completed before next school year starts.

Some parents have mentioned the dangerous crossing at the corner of Milton Street near the school entrance. We have raised this and been told that road alterations will soon make it much safer, but that in the meantime a lollipop lady has been employed.

We should like to remind parents about visits to the parents of new children in the summer. Last year 25 parents volunteered to visit the parents of all children coming into the school to see if they could answer questions and it was very successful and much appreciated. This year we take in a lot of children from the West Exchester estate, and it would be helpful if about 30 parents could help. Mrs Tripp, chairman of the Parents' Association will be asking for volunteers early in the summer term.

Finally we should like to give you early warning that two of us 'retire' at the end of this year, and so anyone wishing to be a parent governor should volunteer when the note about elections comes round. We have enjoyed the work and found it interesting, and we should be glad to tell anyone wishing to stand for election what is involved.

Yours sincerely,

Eileen Chandler
David Evans
Alice Stephenson

61

Remember the point made in Chapter 2 about confidentiality. Make sure that your fellow governors know when you are discussing issues with parents so that no confidences are breached. One further point to remember when soliciting parents' points of view is that it is too easy to report only the views of one's own circle of friends. It is often said that only middle-class parents volunteer for this kind of responsibility, which is partly, if not entirely, true. Thus anyone elected from the posh end of town ought not to report only the views of Rotary wives or opinions gleaned from Tupperware parties or the golf club dinner dance. There is much to be said for parent governors being chosen from different parts of the school's catchment area, and it should be possible for the people elected to be sensitive to views from all sections of the community.

DO — Become known to your constituents.
— Send an occasional newsletter.
— Represent all sections of the community not just your own friends.
— Involve other parents in your work beforehand, not merely tell them about it afterwards.

DON'T — Overplay the line, 'Well my son is in the school, so I got the inside story'. Nudge, nudge, wink, wink.
— Press your own children's case, either openly or craftily, at the expense of others.
— Be afraid to speak if the meeting is full of apparent experts. You are there as the voice of parents, not as Britain's leading authority on curriculum development. Good professionals welcome a clearly expressed non-expert's point of view. In any case many parents are far more expert in their knowledge of children's learning and well-being than they realize themselves. On the other hand don't pretend you're an expert if you are not.

Teachers

Teacher governors can also find themselves in an awkward position. They should become members of the team like everyone else, but they are inescapably employees of the local authority, and may be seen by other governors to be biased in favour of their colleagues whenever anything to do with teaching comes under scrutiny.

Furthermore, as they are also professionally knowledgeable in education they may be tempted to overawe fellow governors with their expertise, and nothing will kill discussion or arouse hostility more quickly.

Their own colleagues will expect to know that their views are represented, and to be consulted about key issues. It is not a bad idea, therefore, for a note to be displayed permanently on the staff notice board giving the names of teacher governors, so that all, especially newcomers, are clear who is acting in this way for them. The same section of notice board can display notes of information for colleagues about what is happening in governors' meetings, though confidentiality should not be breached.

Anyone volunteering to stand as a teacher governor should be clear from the outset about the pressures which may ensue. On a particular issue, for example, the majority of her colleagues may hold one view, which she is duty bound to report, and the head may hold a different view — so already the teacher governor's loyalties are divided. She may herself hold a third view, which she should be as free to express as any other governor present.

As suggested on the section on parent governors above, she should respect confidentiality and try to discover the views of all her colleagues on matters, not just those of her personal friends or like-minded individuals. One way of doing this is to raise appropriate matters at staff meetings, so that both she and the head can try to interpret staff's views. Whilst it is not a bad idea for the head and the teacher governors to consult before governors' meetings, it is not advisable for there to be such powerful collusion that the rest of the group feels threatened by a professional conspiracy.

The teacher governor should not be made to feel by the head that blind unswerving loyalty is demanded irrespective of her own views, and that any mild dissent is a serious breach of professional etiquette. On the other hand the teacher governor should not seek to embarrass the head deliberately, nor to win victories in the governing body denied to her in staff meetings, unless there is a serious problem of disharmony and lack of confidence in the senior people within the school.

When matters to do with individual members of staff are raised, teacher governors often withdraw. (They are sometimes required by the Articles to do so.) It is as well to minimize the occasions when any governor has to withdraw, so that the group can act as a team; and indeed it is an important aspect of professional life that people have to learn to keep a confidence, act fairly and humanely, and not press their own special interest at the expense of their colleagues.

On the other hand when a teacher governor's own affairs or a matter of direct concern to her are being discussed, she should always, in her own interests, be asked to withdraw. Just as a teacher governor should not be granted special privileges because of her position on the governing body, so too she should not be any worse off.

The following summarizes some of the points made above:

DO
— Keep all your colleagues reasonably in the picture, using notice boards and meetings as necessary.
— Represent all views when asked, not merely those of friends or people with whom you agree.
— Express your own point of view, even if it conflicts with the majority view of your colleagues; you have that right the same as anyone else present.
— Discuss first with the head any issue on which you suspect you may wish to disagree with her. You are entitled to hold contrary views but out of courtesy you should let her know if possible.

DON'T
— Dazzle fellow governors with technical jargon. Better to carry your real or imagined expertise lightly. This means avoiding phrases like 'Research has proved that . . .' (it rarely has).
— Feel threatened if one of the parents has a child in your class. Carry on normally.
— Press your own, your best friend's or your department's case unfairly when other colleagues are not present to put a contrary point of view.
— Dismiss the views of the lay people on the governing body. They may be contrary to current orthodoxy, but they should be listened to.
— Feel you have to justify everything the school does. Good schools constantly review their practices. Although other governors might be alarmed if you never had any confidence in what the school was doing, they will understand that issues in education

are not always black and white, and that honest self-doubts can sometimes produce healthy changes.
   — Serve for ever. Allow colleagues to have the experience, even if they wish to re-elect you. It is good for the job to be shared amongst several teachers over the years.

The head

Heads have a vital role to play in any board of governors. Poor relationships between the head and the governing body can affect the running of the whole school and is, fortunately, relatively rare, being usually a symptom of some deeper problem when it occurs. There is everything for the school, and indeed the community, to gain when relationships between head and governors are good.

The head's report is often an important part of the meeting, other governors being very dependent on him to keep them up to date with what is happening. Governors appreciate honesty here, being unconvinced at hearing nothing but games results when everyone knows there are problems elsewhere.

Most governing bodies look to the head for a clear lead on almost every issue which occurs, and it is as well not to be too defensive and try to prevent governors asking searching questions. The 'clever' head who approaches meetings too slickly, because he believes governing bodies are a nonsense and only need proper handling to make them totally innocuous, does himself and his school a disservice. Successful heads involve their governors in the life of the school whilst not for one moment ducking their own responsibilities.

The balance between the paid professionals, hired to take front-line responsibility for running the school, and the governors, unpaid amateurs charged with certain responsibilities and expected to show interest in the school in general, is perhaps a difficult one to strike, but many heads have done it to the satisfaction of all concerned, and without the need for an elaborate rule book or demarcation procedure.

In summary:

DO   — Be open and above board about successes and problems, it will usually be appreciated.

65

- Establish good rapport with the chairman in particular.
- Express your own point of view, even if it conflicts with that of the rest of the staff.
- Encourage governors to be actively involved in the school in some way, not just attend meetings.

DON'T
- Dazzle governors with technical expertise.
- Blackmail the teacher or parent governors by looking hurt if they disagree with your views.
- Feel threatened if governors offer positive suggestions. If they are bad explain why you cannot use them; if they are good seize them with alacrity. No individual has a monopoly of wisdom.
- Boast to your colleagues that you have your governors sewn up. They may grass on you!
- Deride councillors and lay governors. They are trying, in the main, to perform a public service, and are often delighted to be asked for help.

Pupils

When pupils attend governors' meetings as observers, the chief complaint voiced about them is that they rarely join in discussions. Clearly there are difficulties when an experienced adolescent finds herself amongst adults, including her own teacher and head and several leaders in the community.

Nevertheless pupils can and do perform a useful function, and much of what is said above applies to them: that they should try to speak for their fellow pupils not merely give their own point of view, that of their friends or their own age group, and that they should keep other pupils informed about what goes on at governors' meetings, except when this involves confidential matters, although usually they will not have been present for such business.

Teachers should take seriously the role of pupil observer, and, without reducing the pupil's role, help her to do the job properly by explaining about procedure, giving relevant background information and letting her produce a newsletter for the notice board. Handled well the experience can be a piece of sound social education, both for the pupils directly involved and for the whole student body.

Chair

The chair and vice-chair of governors sit in a very important and influential position. They are responsible for setting the tone at meetings, and can be an important lubricant, establishing communication between themselves and the head, and between the governors and the LEA. The role of chair is dealt with more fully in Chapter 4.

Co-opted governors

Some governors are recruited because of a special role they play in the community. They may, for example, be experienced in the world of industry, the church, farming or the social services. They can bring a dimension to the governing body which other members cannot readily give.

It is important that they use their strengths for the benefit of the school. It is useless if someone co-opted from local industry never shows interest, or merely turns up to meetings to air time-honoured prejudices about education. On the other hand someone who forges links with the world of work, advises about building, financial matters or careers, can be a treasure. Employers of co-opted governors can help by allowing their employee some time off and by not docking their salary on the few occasions they may need to take a little time off work for school business.

Administrators

What has been said above about teachers and heads applies to professional administrators, such as Area Education Officers, who attend governors' meetings acting as clerk: they should not overplay the role of 'expert'; not evade issues by exploiting their knowledge of committee procedure or the complexity of County Hall; not dress up their own prejudices by falsely claiming them to be government or county policy. And they should report practice at other schools, not to disparage a particular school but to inform discussion.

Training for governors

There are several ways in which governors can be trained to do their job effectively. Many local authorities have been running workshops for governors for several years, some lasting a half or a whole day, others spread over a residential weekend, or comprising a series of sessions spread over a long period. Courses are sometimes put on for governors over a whole region, or mounted specifically for one or two governing bodies.

There is a great deal to be said for a carefully thought out policy on governor training. Amongst basic principles might be the following:

Involve the profession. Heads or teachers might occasionally be hostile to training programmes if they fantasize that a squad of muscled heavies will descend on them bristling with expertise and tactical weaponry. If one involves heads in the training not only can they see what is happening, but they can give valuable advice.

Make it practical. Let governors see curricular materials, tackle real cases which have come before governors, and role play imaginary meetings. Use problem cases, like those in Chapter 7. Where possible use good video material such as that available from the BBC or the Open University.

Bring in as many as possible. Training courses which only allow one person to attend from each governing body will take an age to spread and will never reach most people. If possible regional courses should be mounted for two or three representatives from each governing body, and local courses for a larger group of people from each school.

Provide back-up material. Often people go to training courses and then find they cannot recall the details. A small resource booklet or pamphlet summarizing the conference, a set of guidelines, letters of information or news sheets will give people a useful record of proceedings to which they can refer at leisure.

Follow through. Often courses are put on and then forgotten about. Governors who have been to an induction course in the early stages of their governorship may have an appetite for something more exacting after a year or two. Furthermore it should be remembered that hundreds of new governors are engaged every year, in many cases for the first time in their lives. Thus a course run one year might have to be repeated every year or two to cater for all the newcomers.

A sample programme for a one-day induction course might look something like this:

9.30	*Introduction: Governors' responsibilities and relationships with the LEA* Mr J. Thomas, Deputy Chief Education Officer
10.15	*Financial matters* Mrs B. Davies, Accountant
11.00	Coffee
11.15	Working groups (lists on notice board) Watch and discuss video on new curriculum initiatives
12.30	Chairs of groups to report back
1.00	Lunch
2.00	Split into two groups for primary and secondary governors A. Recent developments in primary education: Mrs A. Bowles, Head of South Exchester First School B. Recent developments in secondary education: Mrs C. Jackson, Warden of Exchester Teachers' Centre
3.00	Tea
3.15	Discussion groups, deal with case studies A, B and C
4.15	Plenary session
4.45	Conference ends

Heads, university and college lecturers, advisers and experienced governors might act as group chairmen, and the case material provided can be fictitious items based on real events, involving pupil suspensions, teacher misdemeanour, parents appealing against governors' decisions, financial aspects and so on.

Follow-up sessions might subsequently deal with various new curricula, legislation affecting schools, and introduction to County Hall, important national or local reports and any new Education Act.

In addition to courses by LEAs, governors can inform themselves about new developments relevant to their job by showing a lively interest in what is written about education. This point is further developed in Chapter 5 and suggested reading is given in Appendix C.

Lay governors and appointing staff

Governors are also involved in making appointments to the school staff, along, of course, with the headteacher and possibly a specialist adviser from County Hall. This is a most important assignment and we shall therefore discuss it at greater length. There is no need for you as a lay governor to feel that you have nothing to offer the experts. By the time things get as far as the interview, applicants with unsuitable professional qualifications will usually have been sifted out, and the appointment will probably turn around which candidate is likely to fit into the school and make the best contribution to all aspects of school life. Here a well-informed governor can have as much to contribute as the professional experts. On occasion, you might even score a point or two. On one occasion a lay governor, in private life a housewife, asked a very highly qualified applicant for a post teaching Domestic Science why the subject was taught in school at all; after all, wasn't it up to parents to teach their children to cook at home? The candidate appeared not to have faced that basic question before and floundered badly, yet none of the experts present saw fit to ask it.

'Hire in haste, repent at leisure' is an old saying in the appointments business. A teacher may be appointed after an interview of no more than half an hour. He may spend the next twenty years doing untold damage to your school and your hopes. Time spent on the careful selection of a teacher is not wasted.

In general, it is a good thing that governors should be closely involved with new appointments. It is, for example, one way in which you can become involved with what is taught in your school and how. Equally importantly it provides an excellent way of getting to know the teachers. There are unfortunately a number of horror stories around of governors who ask idiotic questions or ride roughshod over the views of others, and such behaviour when it occurs embarrasses all concerned. Governors are now a regular feature of appointing committees, whereas a few years ago many appointments would have been made by heads acting alone.

During the 1980s and 1990s there are large changes in the number of children in secondary schools in particular, and consequently there will be too few or too many teachers for the schools. In order to ease the problem of redundancy, LEAs will do their best to fill teaching vacancies with teachers displaced from other schools within the authority. This could perhaps give you a headache. When a head is told that he must reduce his staff because of falling numbers he will not be keen to lose his best teachers first. He might even be glad to be rid of someone who can be traded off to another school. On the other hand, when the LEA is forced to close down a whole school, you might be able to pick up teachers who will be a real asset to your own school.

Whether the LEA can force you to accept a transfer to fill a vacancy at your school depends on local circumstances. Look carefully at your Articles of Government, and remember that your first responsibility is to the school you govern. There seems to be little point in giving yourself a problem simply in order to solve one of the LEA's! In particular, take the matter up with your clerk, and look at the teachers' Conditions of Employment or the Staff Code for your LEA. The governors of a small rural school in Devon actually appealed to the High Court when they felt the LEA had forced a teacher on them and the LEA withdrew its decision and appointed someone else.

We return to the question of school closures and falling rolls in Chapter 6.

When a vacancy occurs

If you are asked to assist in the appointment of a new teacher, you should first discuss with the head what the vacancy actually is, and find out her ideas on the sort of qualifications and person she would like. Your options might be limited: if the need is to replace the one and only teacher of knitting, because pupils are half-way through an examination course, then there is no room to manoeuvre. However, if the vacancy is within a large department it might be possible to work in something new – say, Computer Studies in the Mathematics department, or Russian in Modern Languages. You might even find it possible to start a new out-of-school activity with the assistance of the person you appoint. Teachers in primary schools are usually generalists, i.e. they teach a range of class subjects. In secondary schools they are usually subject specialists teaching History, Science and so on. In our rapidly changing society it is often important that teachers should be flexible, and an ability to teach as part of an integrated studies team in Humanities or Environmental Studies may be very useful.

You should also find out any other factors involved in making the new appointment. The school may need, perhaps, more women teachers to even up the burden of those school duties which can be done only by a member of a particular sex, though unless the work can only be carried out by a person of that sex, the Sex Discrimination Act does not allow employers to appoint or reject people on the grounds of their sex alone. The post might be more suitable for an experienced teacher if it involves difficult children, otherwise a keen young teacher straight from college or university might be just what you want. Perhaps the department needs some vigorous new ideas injecting into it, and so on.

Candidates for appointment always appreciate being given the opportunity to have a good look at the school and their prospective colleagues before they take a post. The best method is usually to hold interviews later in the day, and make it possible for the interviewees to spend the earlier part of the day looking around and generally talking to people. This arrangement pays handsome dividends, since some applicants who might have accepted the post on interview find that your school is really not for them and save everybody much wasted time.

Finally, look through the application forms of those to be interviewed in advance. Remember that they are personal and highly confidential documents, and intended solely for the interviewers. If you are in doubt as to what parts of them mean, ask the head to explain.

Do's and Don'ts at the interview

Here are a few suggestions. Allow the candidate to talk, and don't talk too much yourself. Find out what else, apart from his main subjects, the candidate has to offer your school. Games? Chess? Producing a school play? Stay away from discussing the candidate's politics or religion. Of course, if you are appointing a Religious Education teacher in a voluntary school (or, indeed, any teacher in a denominational school) it is permissible to question a candidate about his religious opinions and practice. Remember the Race Relations and Equal Opportunities Acts make it illegal to consider the racial origin or, generally, sex of applicants. Ask the candidate what he makes of your school after looking around. If he has nothing to say, he may either be not very wide awake or, worse, a creep.

Find out what he has discovered about the school in general before he came to interview. This will give some indication of how interested he is in your particular post.

Ask him to talk about his achievements in his present post. Ask him to say why he thinks his subject should be taught in school instead of, say, learning to drive or snake-charming.

If the candidate has had several posts, ask why. Perhaps he has conscientiously set out to gain wide experience, which is a good thing, particularly if you are looking for a senior appointment. On the other hand it may mean that he never stays long enough to be rumbled, and may well leave you quickly too.

Watch out for outdated qualifications. A 'Distinction' on a college course, or a first-class degree mean little if the holder has done little since he gained them ten years ago or more. Teachers, like doctors, should keep up with new developments in their field through further training courses, which are readily available if teachers are willing to invest their time and show interest. Beware of the 'I'm far too conscientious to leave my pupils to go on courses' argument: if top surgeons took that view many of us would now be dead.

Read the references supplied carefully. It is often worthwhile to check that the most obvious people have been asked to support the application. Although an applicant is perfectly free to ask whomsoever he likes to act as his referee, it is clearly odd, for example, if a teacher quotes only the pub landlord and his uncle in ICI. If you have doubts on this score, ask the applicant during the interview.

Ask what the candidate would do in your school if he had a free hand. Ask him how he would provide in his teaching for the cleverest and weakest children. Find out his attitude to punishment and incentives for children.

Finally, always allow sufficient time at the end for the candidate to ask you any questions he may have. Appointments are a two-way process, and the candidate is entitled to interview the school, although people who do this too aggressively often irritate the interviewers.

Remember that if you are asked to take part in an appointment it is one of the most important tasks you will have to do as a governor. Remember, too, that the people coming for interview are usually highly trained professionals who may have to uproot their family if you appoint them, and who may have travelled a considerable distance to attend for interviews. Interviews should be searching but sensitive affairs.

Helping the school

We asked a number of heads how governors had been particularly helpful to their school. We heard many stories of good support, and this was particularly marked when governors, despite their different backgrounds, acted as a supportive team rather than as a set of disparate individuals.

They told us of parent governors who mobilized other parents to visit the houses of new pupils; of business governors who persuaded their colleagues to provide work experience, raised money to help finance pupils' projects, or helped arrange mock interviews for older students about to enter the job market; of political governors who took on County Hall and their own political party; of governors who came along to school-based in-service courses to see what was new in education; of those who supported the school in the face of a malicious newspaper report.

The other side of the coin is equally illuminating. Governors spoke appreciatively of heads who kept them in the picture, of local authorities who put on interesting courses, of teachers who were open and honest about successes and problems and did not put obstacles in the way of governors trying to do their job.

Sadly there was also a negative element. Heads told of governors who rarely appeared and then torpedoed whatever was suggested; of the governor who opposed the head's release for an in-service course on the grounds that heads should already know all there is to know; the one who stormed into the school announcing she had just been made a governor and had come to inspect; the governor who insisted on helping in the classroom and bored the class to tears with long-winded stories; the one who, because he was a lawyer, claimed expertise on everything on the agenda; and a number of bad chairs who ruled autocratically, failed to take advice and were insensitive to nervous parent or lay members.

Unhappy stories from governors concerned, for example, the head who constantly reminded them that they knew little about education and that he was really in charge, or who said he would consider each suggestion and then quietly forgot about it; the teacher governor who saw every proposal as an attack on the profession, the administrator who never gave an opinion, but always said he would have to consult his colleagues or the great Chief Education Officer in the sky, and the local authority who kept telling governors how important they were, but never gave any direct help or advice.

In general, however, there were many happy stories, a few miserable ones and some total catastrophes. The greatest enemy appeared to be apathy. Fairly frequently people reported that their governing body had gone into a cosy rut, turning up for tea, cakes and chat, and going cheerfully on their way, uncertain why they had met, and sometimes feeling the only purpose had been to plan the time and date of the next meeting and hear yet again that the boys' toilets needed repairing.

There is an important and valuable function for school governors to fulfil and it is the collective duty of all the governing body, not just the head and chairman, to see that the job is done sensitively, constructively and effectively. Whilst commonsense and goodwill alone will not ensure this, they will certainly lay a sound foundation. Anyone uneasy or uncertain about what the governors are doing can always ask the chair to allow a discussion of how the governors can best conduct their business to be a central item on the agenda.

4

Governors' meetings

What is a committee?

'Through you, Madam Chairman', 'Is there a seconder for the motion?', 'I'm sorry but I must rule that out of order'. People joining a committee for the first time are often surprised and even intimidated by the formality of language employed by members who, a few minutes earlier, were perhaps convulsing each other with risqué stories, or calling one another Sid, Dick and Mary. There is thus a need for members of a governing body, particularly those who have not been in such a group before, to become familiar with committee procedure.

A committee is a group of people who meet occasionally or regularly to discuss matters in a certain field. It may be *executive*, i.e. able to make and possibly enforce decisions, or *advisory*. Most committees have been set up by some larger group of people and are therefore accountable to that group. Like governing bodies of schools they may be both executive and advisory, given delegated powers to make some decisions without reference back to the larger group, in this case the LEA, but frequently acting in an advisory capacity. It is often when a committee exceeds its powers that problems are created.

This pattern can be extended still further. Most committees will at some time set up an even smaller group of themselves as a *sub-committee* to do a particular job for which the larger group might be too cumbersome. The sub-committee will then report back to the main committee. In governing bodies this typically happens over matters like staff appointments.

Certain assumptions are made about committees. They are not always fulfilled but can be described as general unwritten hopes when committees assemble. First of all it is assumed that business will be conducted in an *orderly* manner. Anyone who has ever been to a chaotic or acrimonious meeting will know how important orderliness can be. A committee will usually, therefore, have certain agreed procedures to ensure the smooth transaction of its affairs. It will have an *agenda* listing items of business, sometimes with supporting papers giving members background information; a *chair* who will organize the meeting, call on speakers, give a ruling when necessary, sum up, decide when to pass on to the next item and so on; and a *secretary* to make the notes which will eventually constitute the record of that meeting.

Secondly, because decisions often have to be made, it will be assumed that after discussion a *consensus* of members' views will be sought. If there is some doubt it may be desirable to put the matter to a vote. Again the common assumption is that members will agree to abide by the majority decision and that if there is deadlock the chair will give a casting vote.

Thirdly, there should be a sense of *collective responsibility*, that is an agreement that, once a decision is made, members will not thereafter publicly dissociate themselves from it, but rather support it as a group, even if they themselves were against it in discussion. This convention is frequently broken, especially when an individual member feels especially strongly about some matter, or is mandated by the group he represents to advocate a particular point of view. If, for example, many parents press a parent governor to raise an issue which is subsequently defeated when put to the vote, it would be most unfair if that governor had to pretend that he totally approved of the decision. On the other hand, in the interest of group cohesion he should not be publicly aggressive about his disagreement, otherwise the governors cannot function as a unit, only as a collection of individuals or pressure groups. The best solution is probably for the dissenting governor to have his dissent recorded in the public minutes of the meeting.

Other conventions are also broken at times, for either good or bad reasons. Someone wishing to undermine a group may seek to have business conducted in a *disorderly* manner by constant interruption, refusal to accept the chair's rulings, or by speaking at excessive length. This kind of roguish inability to accept reasonable chairmanship is quite rare, and when it does occur sometimes suggests that the chairmanship has been unreasonable.

Committee procedure

To avoid people quarrelling with each other across the room remarks are normally addressed 'through the chair'. This can sometimes reduce acrimony. For example, the angry exchange:

> *Speaker A* I never said you twisted the account of the last meeting.
> *Speaker B* Yes you did, you liar.

might, in strict committee language, go something like:

> *Speaker A* I wonder, Mr Chairman, if Mr Bloggs could clarify what he felt was wrong with the version of events just given.
> *Chairman* Mr Bloggs, could you tell us a bit more about your objection?
> *Speaker B* I felt that minute 234 was not entirely accurate and should have read . . .

Skilful 'Black Belt' committee members can still use committee procedure to generate hostility, anger or to scapegoat, and no amount of formal chairmanship will ever make a miserable group happy or a divided group cohesive. The question of formality is discussed again below.

In order that members may make their decisions and recommendations in the best possible circumstances, certain features of committee work are essential. First of all the location is important. Frequently meetings take place in dismal or cramped conditions, and it is impossible to avoid an air of seediness about the whole affair. Governors should be able to sit in reasonable comfort, neither perched precariously on infant-sized stools nor submerged in the sumptuous and sleep-inducing armchairs of the Alderman Harry Ramsbottom Committee Room.

"I'LL PUT MR. JONES DOWN
AS AN ABSTENTION ON THIS ONE"

The room should be decently lit and ventilated, so that members do not have to share the same limited supply of oxygen, and they should agree not to have dined too well beforehand. Those who do so may lapse into slumber, which is not good for the chairman's morale, and they should be awakened unless elderly, frail or more effective asleep than awake, as their eventual loud snore might turn out to be the decisive vote on an important item.

Certain bits of paraphernalia go with meetings. Most important of these are 'the papers', a twentieth-century form of magic, which incorporate the business of the meeting.

Minutes and agenda

Two vital pieces of paper are needed at each meeting. First of all there are the minutes of the last meeting, the record kept by the secretary of business transacted, usually in numbered form:

Minute 234   Head's report

The head reported on the period 1st April to 31st July (copy filed with minutes). Members noted with pleasure the growing interest in charity work and asked the head to convey their congratulations to the pupils and teachers involved. There was some discussion of the amount of time required to administer the GCSE examination. Governors expressed their regret at the low take-up of a second or alternative foreign language in the current 3rd year, but were glad to note that the staff were very concerned and were taking action to see that more information would be given to pupils and parents about the choices available.

Minutes of meetings are kept together as a permanent record of the life of the school, and some schools have accounts of such meetings going back for hundreds of years. Consequently it is important that the minutes should be accurate. Governors should not hesitate to point out inaccuracies, unless these are tiny and immaterial, but it is not fair for members of a committee to insist that each of their own contributions and every brilliant turn of phrase be logged in. The minuting secretary has a difficult task encapsulating the spirit of perhaps twenty minutes of discussion into five or six lines without being harangued for omitting 'the bit where I said how important it was for the locker-room cupboard to be installed by Christmas'.

If everyone wants his own name in lights the minutes become not a record of the meeting but a literal transcript of it. A word for word transcript of a two hour meeting could run to 20 or 30 pages, would invade nobody's bestseller list, and would lead to even more Norwegian forests biting the dust to provide the paper. The best one should expect from a set of minutes is a brief and accurate account, giving the flavour of the meeting and recording any decisions taken.

The agenda for a meeting represents the batting order of items to be discussed. Certain time-honoured features regularly appear. A typical agenda, missing out the middle, might look something like this:

Meeting of school governors to be held on Thursday April 27th at 7 p.m. in the quiet reading room of the school library.

AGENDA
1. *Apologies for absence*
2. *Minutes of last meeting* (February 10th)
3. *Matters arising*
    (a) *Minute 234* Outcome of staff meetings on 3rd year options (Head to report)
    (b) *Minute 236* Deputation to County Hall on March 13th (Mr Jones to report)

(c) *Minute 241* Delays to Cloakroom extension in south wing (Chair to report)

4. *Head's report*

5. *New housing estate in West Exchester* Governors will know that planning permission has now been granted for Messrs Botchett and Scarper to build 75 three- and four-bedroomed houses in West Exchester. A paper from the Chief Education Officer explaining possible implications for the school is attached.

   . . . etc.

12. *Date and time of next meeting*
Thursday July 13th at 7 p.m. is proposed.

13. *Any other business*

Usually the chair will begin by asking if members agree that the minutes of the last meeting constitute a correct record of events. He signs the filed copy when this is agreed, having made any necessary alterations first. 'Matters arising' allows the chair or any other member to update colleagues on the latest state of whatever was discussed last time. Sometimes certain matters for report are already included in the agenda, and members are then invited to comment on other relevant items as they wish. Unless there is a particularly pressing 'matter arising' the group normally passes fairly quickly on to the main body of the agenda, otherwise the meeting can never get itself moving ahead.

Newcomers to committee work never understand how the agenda is assembled. Some secretaries or chairs of committees circulate members in advance asking if there is anything they wish to raise, others assemble the agenda themselves. It is wise to make known how members may introduce an item, the deadline date for typing and distribution and so on, otherwise a sense of frustration develops, or else thorny issues are introduced unexpectedly under 'any other business'.

If you, as a governor, wish to raise an issue it might be helpful to provide a short paper to support the case. People are sometimes unnecessarily inhibited when asked to provide a paper, assuming that a great literary masterpiece is essential, or alternatively that a lengthy document with footnotes and tables is required. A supporting paper is often quite brief, and serves simply to let other members know in advance what the item is about. For example if an item appears as:

6. *School uniform*

no-one knows what is involved. Is there some move to abolish it? Do people wish to change the style of uniform? On the other hand if the item appears as:

6. *School uniform* (paper from Mrs Jenkins attached)

and a short covering note in simple, plain language from Mrs Jenkins is available, like the one below, governors both know what is to be discussed and can find information or think of ideas in advance.

School uniform

At a recent PTA Meeting the question of the high cost of school uniform was raised. Parents were not against school uniform, but were worried at the expense involved, particularly to parents with two or three children at the school. The head and staff were very sympathetic, and we agreed that it should be given some thought before next year. One possibility was that any red cardigan or jumper should be allowed, not just the expensive ribbed one. Another suggestion was that we might somehow help parents buy second-hand uniforms from each other. One person thought that a grant was available to help parents with a low income, but no-one seemed sure. Knowing that one governor was a social worker and another a teacher at a school that had tackled the problem already, we thought it would be a good idea if I, as a parent governor, raised it at a governors' meeting. Both the head and chair have agreed to this so I hope we can spend a few minutes on it. The head and PTA committee have said they are quite happy to look at any suggestions which come from this meeting.

Edna Jenkins

For similar reasons when items come from the head or the Chief Education Officer they frequently have a paper attached, and governors should become familiar with the background to each item before the event. The only situation worse than a meeting where some members have clearly not even glanced at the papers, is when the chair is in this position.

Sometimes the item 'any other business' does not feature in an agenda. This is because members may in the past have raised controversial matters under this heading late in a meeting, with

82

no-one in possession of the appropriate information. If a member wishes to raise something, whether under this heading or not, after the agenda has appeared, it is customary to ask the chair's permission in advance. He may then rule whether it is appropriate to take it at such late notice or whether it should be deferred until the next meeting. In fairness to all other governors, members should try their best to have all important items put on the agenda in the proper way and in good time. If someone tries to bring up an important matter under 'any other business' when several members have already left, propose that it be deferred until the next meeting. Some LEAs have been known to leave 'any other business' off their agendas so that the ruling party caucus can discuss their 'line' on all matters before governors' meetings. Object to this loudly and longly!

Reaching decisions

Some items on the agenda need a decision and others merely require an airing. When a firm decision is needed it is common for the chair to interpret the mood of the meeting. Where there has been clear agreement the chair will often ask 'Do we agree then that . . .?' or 'Am I right in assuming that no-one is in favour of . . .?' Where the feeling of the meeting is not clear-cut a vote is usually taken.

Formal procedure over voting can sometimes become a little complex. Normally members will be told what they are voting on, and if anyone is not clear what the issue is he should ask for a statement from the chair. Normal committee procedure requires one member to propose a motion and another to 'second' it. Once the wording has been agreed the chair will ask for a vote: 'All those in favour please show . . . all those against . . . abstention . . . I declare the motion carried by 12 votes to 8 with 2 abstentions.'

Life becomes complex when members disagree over the wording of a motion and wish to propose amendments. Thus someone may say, 'I disagree with the motion as put, could we vote on an amended version and add the phrase "provided he has not made a request during the previous twelve months"?' If a seconder is found the chair will usually put the amendment to a vote first to see if it is acceptable or if members prefer the original motion. It is up to members of a committee to make sure that such constitutional matters do not become silly. Most governors want to discuss issues of concern, not to train as barristers.

It is the chair's duty to make sure that any formal proposal is clearly worded, not saturated with negatives and ambiguities. Most people operating at sub-genius level would not be certain what a 'Yes' or 'No' vote means with a motion such as 'we deplore anyone refusing to do nothing'. It is far better to vote on a positive version of a motion so that those voting 'for' or 'against' are crystal clear about what they are supporting.

Once a vote has been taken the strength of the voting is often important. A group will have more confidence if the vote was clear cut than if it was close. When the voting results in a tie the chair may give a second, or casting, vote. Some chairs always give a casting vote *against* any change on the grounds that a tie does not constitute a majority in favour of change and things should therefore stay as they are. This stance is only really justifiable, if at all, if the chair has no strong feelings on the issue. The chair is usually an important person and if he has any views at all he should not hesitate to air them. The risk that some unpopular issue might become widely known as having been approved 'only on the chair's casting vote' is one of the hazards a chair must occasionally face up to when agreeing to take on the assignment. He can be reassured that chairs universally have to take on such responsibility, and that it is relatively rare for the casting vote to be needed. No-one should castigate a chair for exercising his duty to resolve a dead-lock.

Group dynamics

There is something about the chemistry of a group of people meeting together which defies perfect explanation, even though a great deal of work has been undertaken studying such groups. Studies of group dynamics are far too numerous to mention here, but some aspects are of interest.

Small group dynamics are different from large group dynamics. In larger groups people will often have less time to speak and there will be more silent members. Some participants will be under pressure to utter views they do not really support because they are aware that it is sometimes more important to have been seen to state a point of view than actually to believe in it. For example, a parent governor might have to voice 'the parental view' whilst privately disagreeing with it. Smaller groups are usually much more informal and decisions are negotiated more casually. Few family breakfasts involve someone proposing and seconding a motion of censure on whoever buttered the toast.

Studies of groups have shown that people frequently play a regular and predictable role in them. There is often a social welfare person who switches on lights, turns heating up or down, suggests it must be time for coffee or that a window needs opening. A joker can help relieve tension by making people smile, or occasionally heighten it when his funnies misfire. A guardian of the nation's morals may remind members that doom is around the corner, that levity will not do, and that sombre faces should be the order of the day. An aura of perpetual sin hangs round such a person, contaminating the rest of the group who feel guilty without being able to say why. A brisk and businesslike efficiency expert may always be hustling the chair on to the next item. There are many other stereotypes.

Similarly in some groups people regularly have an expectation of time, and often fill it with remarkable accuracy. If eight people meet regularly for an hour, one may talk for twenty minutes, another for ten, yet another remain silent. If for some reason the twenty-minute person is silent for the first half hour he is then under considerable pressure to dominate the last half hour and obtain his ration of talk.

Position in the room or around the table is also a feature of many groups. Without realizing it, people who disagree with each other frequently choose places opposite one another and avoid adjacent seats, on the grounds that it is very difficult to sustain an argument with someone sitting at your left ear. Similarly those who share views often sit together and a concerted and sometimes orchestrated set of arguments for or against an issue will appear stronger coming from a cohesive group of three or four people. On the other hand, super-shrewd operators sometimes deliberately seat themselves in different places around a table so that an impression of general group agreement on an issue is created.

Why some groups manage beautifully and others never get off the ground is very difficult to explain. Certain features which kill groups stone dead are well known. One very aggressive member can spoil meetings and sensitive individuals subjected to a personal attack from such a person may never reappear or rarely speak thereafter. Amongst killers of good group interaction are

85

the following stereotypes. Although caricatures, they are alive and well and often do not readily respond to hints, though you could try circling the appropriate description in this section of the book and leaving it open at the culprit's seat with a note signed 'A friend'.

The bad listener never hears what others say because he is only waiting for a gap in the discussion to enable him to make his own contribution. This frequently is a repetition of what someone has already said.

The 'expert' can be a pain in the neck, particularly if he is not really an expert at all. The person who once built himself a back porch should not pronounce loftily on all building matters, particularly if it fell down. One governing body had to suffer the pontifications of an elderly lawyer. As the sole university graduate in the group he constantly spoke inaccurately on examinations or further and higher education from the basis of hopelessly out of date memories of his own early days. Even real experts can inhibit discussion by appearing to rule on every topic, but fortunately many genuine experts carry their learning lightly and do not overpower their fellows. Perhaps some of the worst offenders, unwittingly, are governors who are teachers at another school, and seek to make the school a replica of their own. A good and sensitive 'expert' on the other hand, whose views are valued by others, can be absolutely invaluable.

The Mona Lisa. People who sit silently throughout meetings wearing an enigmatic look simply put pressure on others to do all the talking. It is refreshing to have members who do not waste words, but governors who never say a single word on any issue for meeting after meeting are often making little contribution unless they are active behind the scenes. Better is an occasional well thought out statement at the appropriate time.

The windbag can be a serious problem because he prevents others from speaking by enjoying his own contributions so much that he never shuts up. All governors may make a lengthy contribution or series of statements at some time or other, but this is not windbaggery. What distinguishes the windbag is that his speeches are repetitive and tedious, often rambling off the point. Skilful chairs have a number of strategies to handle the situation, but even 'May I just interrupt you a second and ask you to sum up?' can spark of another fifteen minutes.

'Little me' uses disarming statements like, 'Well, of course, I don't really know anything about these matters', and then,

having spent all night in the reference library, goes on to reel off DES statistics for the last twenty-five years.

'The Hear! Hear!' Usually half asleep. Says it indiscriminately, often inconsistently, nearly always after someone has spoken loudly.

Finally it should be said that when group dynamics go wrong it is the duty of every member of the governing body to make the group work. Rather than sit back lamenting about what a poor meeting it was, not speak because the level of debate is too low, or grumble about the boring agenda or lack of action, every member can help make a group a success. It should not be left to the chair alone to reduce acrimony, curtail rambling discussions or handle difficult members. If every person present exercises self-discipline, cares about the group and the school it serves, and acts unselfishly and in good faith, there will be few insoluble problems. Indeed, it is a testimony to the basic commonsense of the human race that most governing bodies are friendly and informal. The only reason that there is some concern in this section about problems is that happy groups will run themselves and problem-ridden groups need help.

The chair

The role of the chair in any committee is crucial. She sets the tone of the meeting, decides priorities, steers the group through the business and liaises with the head and LEA. No-one should agree to take on chairmanship of a governing body unless she is willing to work hard to make a success of the job. It is also for stayers and not sprinters.

Many of the problems described above are avoided by skilful chairmanship, yet there are as many different styles of chairing meetings as there are chairs. The first aspect of chairmanship which should be of concern is that it offers considerable power to use or misuse. Thus the effective chairman should be seen to be fair. That is not to say that she may not hold personal views, perhaps strong on some issues, but rather that her personal prejudices should not prevent her from listening to all sides of an argument and giving everyone a chance to contribute.

An autocratic style of chairmanship irritates members considerably. One powerful chair, whose style made Attila the Hun look like a moderate, once took a vote on an issue. There were twenty people present. 'All those in favour?' he asked. Nineteen hands went up. 'Well I'm against it' he rejoined, and passed on to the next item.

"WELL, I'M AGAINST IT, MOTION DEFEATED"

One important choice for the chair is whether meetings should be formal or informal. If there is likely to be strife it is usually better to be formal and insist on contributions 'through the chair'. More often in governing bodies, however, an informal style is preferred. People frequently know each other already or feel more welcome in an informal atmosphere, especially if they are lay people unused to committee work. On the other hand informality does not imply sloppiness. If decisions have to be made and recorded then a certain formality of procedure is necessary, one cannot rely entirely on folk memory.

A good chair can perform several useful services. These include the following:

Pacing. If an agenda has ten or fifteen items she can consult with the headmaster and clerk, using her judgement to see which seem to be important and which seem more trivial. Thus she might start by saying, 'Looking at the agenda it seems as if items 1, 2, 3 and 4 can be dealt with fairly quickly and items 5 and 8 ought to take a little bit more time. If people agree I propose we spend most of our time on items 6 and 7.' At this point members can indicate if they accord with this view, and someone will be free to suggest some other item as a high priority. The advantage of this approach is that it signals to the group where their efforts should be placed, so that they can help the chair move quickly through trivial items, and then debate more thoroughly the key issues. This avoids the problem of spending so long on early matters that later items which are important never receive proper attention. An alternative to this approach is not to make any decisions on priorities but keep a constant eye on the clock reminding people that 'we only have 40 minutes left and still five more items to cover'.

Summing up. Often discussion becomes diffuse and difficult to follow. A good chair can help members considerably by giving an economical and fair summary, preferably from notes she has been keeping. She might, therefore, once in a while, say something like, 'Now is this a fair summary of what people have been saying? Most speakers seemed to be in favour of a small deputation to County Hall, but Mrs French was against that because of our experience last time. On the other hand three or four people thought that if we held a public meeting first and then went to County Hall this would be better than last time when we hadn't prepared our case properly.' Other members can correct this version or agree that it is a fair condensation of discussion to date. A good summary at an appropriate moment can often get a meeting out of a quagmire and move the group nearer a decision.

Ruling. There are frequently moments of uncertainty in committee meetings when people look to the chair for guidance. This requires her to give a ruling on some matter, as when someone says, for example, 'I know we're supposed to be discussing the county document on health education, but can we go back to that previous circular on sex equality or would you rule that out of order?' At this point the chair must use her judgement. Amongst many alternatives might be:

'No, I think we've spent enough time on that issue.'

'Well only for five minutes at the most as we have rather a lot of business still to do.'

'Yes I think that would be well worthwhile.'

'Would members like to spend a little time on that or should we press on?'

'Perhaps the head and the Area Education Officer can advise us on this one.'

'Is there some particular point you wish to bring out briefly about the other circular?'

There are many other possibilities. Provided that the chair is sensitive to the mood of the meeting most committees will accept a fair verdict, and even go along with an unpopular one, realizing that business could never be transacted unless someone ruled on tricky matters. Chairs who run into difficulties have either been too heavy-handed or unsympathetic in their decisions, or else have dithered endlessly when everyone is quite happy to abide by a decision from the chair.

Manoeuvring. Most committees are clean and above board, some are riddled by chicanery. Sometimes it is hard to draw the line distinguishing socially acceptable manoeuvring from dirty tricks. Amongst many time-honoured tricks of the trade, recognizable and easily rumbled if decently handled, annoying and divisive if malevolently done, are the following:

Lobbying. When a person wishes to press a particular point of view he may rally support for it before the meeting. Usually this is a fairly honest procedure; and someone approaches a fellow member saying, 'At the next meeting I'm hoping to persuade members to take some action over what I think is a very pressing problem. If I can just explain the background to you I hope you'll support me.' Occasionally the lobbying is more subtle or even obscure and certain dense, or for that matter shrewd, members of committees can sometimes accrue a fair number of free meals and drinks by not catching on quickly. Indeed if lobbying were made an indictable offence tomorrow a sizeable group of exclusive clubs, pubs and expensive restaurants might go out of business. Too much lobbying reduces the spontaneity of meetings and also sometimes embarrasses members who feel obliged to support people when approached in this way so as not to let them down.

Caucus. When a group of like-minded people wishes to press a particular point of view or secure a certain decision, they sometimes meet as a group before the main committee meeting, and work out a plan of action. This is a fairly common occurrence, but it can be divisive, and it is often better to risk the spontaneity

"I SEE THERE'S BEEN A CAUCUS MEETING AGAIN"

of unrehearsed meetings. For example if the parent governors, the political nominees, the co-opted governors or the head and teacher governors concert their strategies in advance it will be very difficult for the governing body ever to become a cohesive group. Also there is some sourness when the caucus group is in the majority, and non-caucus members find they have little to offer as decisions have been negotiated in advance.

Delaying. Sometimes people in a committee will delay the meeting deliberately to avoid discussion of a controversial item or to ensure fatigue and/or dwindled numbers when an important point is reached. Occasionally a chair will allow the group to dawdle over earlier items to cut short discussion of key later ones. It is up to other members of the group to be alert to this and ask if progress can be a little faster to ensure proper discussion of later items. Another common device is to set up a sub-committee and hope the problem will quietly be buried. Sub-committees should be used to do a proper job, not to dispose of something in an underhand way.

Horse-trading. When individuals or groups known to favour certain points of view are in conflict they will sometimes agree to do a deal in advance. One group will soft-pedal on one issue, the other on a subsequent one, thus allowing both groups some success. This is often totally bewildering and annoying to members of neither group who are utterly baffled by the lack of bite over what have previously been controversial matters.

Dirty versions of the above devices are really not necessary in

91

any properly run committee, and indeed they bring great discredit to the notion of democratic involvement in decision-making. Judicious use of some of the tactics may be acceptable, but any governing body whose members obtain more satisfaction and pleasure from political manoeuvring than from properly looking after the welfare of a school and its community should stop and question why it exists.

Making effective use of committees

Committees are often so stuck with the standard rituals they fail to exploit alternatives to battling through the agenda for session upon session. There are several quite simple and effective ways of conducting business which involve but minor amendments of normal procedures. A skilful chair can ensure that variety in practice makes meetings both interesting and enjoyable.

Buzz groups. Some members of a larger group experience frustration at not having an opportunity to speak. One way of releasing this tension is for the chair to allow the group to dissolve into buzz groups. At its simplest the meeting will be suspended for ten minutes or so whilst people gossip with their immediate neighbours without leaving their seats. Alternatively the chair may say, 'This is an important matter and everyone should have a chance to speak. Let's split into three groups of about six people and come back in half an hour. Perhaps one person in each group will report back when we re-assemble.'

Working parties. When a committee has a particular job to do it may set up a working party to guide it in its thinking. Whereas sub-committees tend to be more permanent, working parties offer flexibility. Three or four people can be asked to meet fairly often to devise a solution to a problem or to fashion a proposal. Eventually they can present a report to the main committee at which point, their job completed, they may cease to exist. The ultimate fate of a successful working party is to be made a sub-committee and live on indefinitely, like the characters in Sartre's *Huis Clos* who thought they were waiting to go to hell and eventually realized they were in it already, condemned to spend eternity in each other's company. At their best, working parties can do an excellent job in a way that a full committee never could.

Day conference. Committee members often feel fatigued particularly if they meet at the end of the day. Once in a while it is worth trying to find a whole day if this can be arranged. This can have a freshness about it, and also allow more time for members to reflect on issues. It is also good for group morale. A typical day's programme, using local resources, might look like this:

	Theme: Changes during the coming year
10 a.m.	Assemble for coffee
10.15	*Some changes the school faces* The head
11.15	Discussion in groups
12.30	Lunch
1.30	*Integrating children with special educational needs* Mr Jackson, Special Needs Adviser
2.15	Discussion in groups
3.00	*The new technology guidelines, resource implications* Mrs Thomas, Science and Technology Co-ordinator
4.00	Tea

Brainstorming. One way out of difficulty when a group has a problem and appears unable to reach a solution is to have a brainstorming session. The rules are very simple. Each member must produce as many ideas as possible, no criticism is allowed, and the secretary writes them all down. Finally all the ideas are considered more critically and any useful ones are adopted. The reason why a brainstorming session can sometimes, though not always, resolve a problem is simply explained. Some quite useful ideas often never reach fruition because they are criticized and discarded too early. Furthermore sometimes a great leap sideways is needed and solutions which initially seem silly can often be just what is needed. Think, for example, of all those early attempts to make aeroplanes. They failed because designers were stuck with the notion of birds and flapping wings. The idea of rigid wings or no wings at all would have seemed nonsense to people at the time, but this was precisely the solution needed.

Action notes. Often in meetings decisions are reached but no action ensues. It is easy for the secretary to the committee to devise a simple action note and send it to anyone who was asked in the meeting to undertake some task. This reminds the person concerned what was agreed. A simple example would be:

Action note (minute 234 – Financial management formula)

You will recall that you agreed at the last governors' meeting to write to the Chief Education Officer on behalf of the governors requesting him or his representative to meet a small deputation before the end of February if possible.

Governors' meetings, like any committee, can be tedious, interesting, pointless or fruitful. Given goodwill and a little ingenuity there is no reason why your own meetings should not be both satisfying and worthwhile. Governors have an important job to do, and if they can get the chemistry of their meetings right they are well on the way to doing it effectively.

5

Life in school

Wherever we have organized short courses for school governors, some of the most popular sessions were about life in school. Afterwards several governors who were not teachers commented freely how ignorant they felt about what was happening in schools, and how much they welcomed the opportunity to hear an up-to-date account and be able to ask questions. 'I sit through meetings', said one parent governor,' knowing little or nothing about several of the things we discuss'. Governors are usually reluctant to stop meetings so that someone can explain GCSE, profiling, the role of the LEA, or whatever.

Indeed several governors with long service on governing bodies or the Education Committee also confessed that, although they had picked up considerable information over the years, the world of education seemed to change so rapidly that it proved impossible for a lay person to keep abreast of recent developments.

Even professionals working in schools, teacher training, the inspectorate or advisory service find it difficult to maintain a firm grasp of all that is going on, but there are several sources of help available to both professionals and lay people. First of all many newspapers employ an education correspondent, and most of these, despite the occasional dud, perform a valuable service bringing stories about reports on education, new ideas in teaching or problems in schools to the attention of a wide readership. Popular magazines often feature educational topics or offer an advisory service.

Television and radio also report educational matters extensively, and programmes such as *Panorama*, *Horizon* and *World in Action* will often cover an issue in some depth with well filmed classroom scenes and usually, though not always, with a fair degree of objectivity. Many local and national radio programmes offer listeners a phone-in opportunity on educational matters from time to time. It is worth watching some of the many programmes for teachers on new developments in schools, or even occasionally sampling schools' television programmes or radio broadcasts, which frequently mirror the best of what is happening in both the primary and secondary sectors.

A further source of information is to be found in the many reasonably priced paperbacks on education, some written especially for parents or anyone interested in schools. Alternatively certain specialist magazines and periodicals appear regularly, and pamphlets are sometimes produced by various agencies, including the DES and local authorities, to give a pithy digest of some important new development on current issues to the general public. A selection of these is given in the bibliography. You can also ask to see copies of the many county circulars which are sent to schools.

Consequently this and the following chapter are only intended to give the reader a flavour of what is happening in primary and secondary schools, and to describe some of the issues and problems being faced by teachers and pupils. In view of the vastness of the area they can be but a starting point.

Changes in society

Many changes in school represent a response to changes in our society of which there have been many in recent times. Children leaving school in the last decade of the twentieth century will need more skills than any previous generation of pupils. There are several reasons for this.

One major reason is the disappearance of millions of unskilled jobs in the 1970s and 1980s. When we read about a multimillion pound investment scheme in industry it will usually obliterate unskilled jobs by the thousand. Tasks that were formerly undertaken by a large cohort of untrained and unskilled workers will in future be done by a small number of highly schooled technocrats, a squad of skilled and semi-skilled personnel, a sizeable group of bureaucrats responsible for paperwork, stock control, ordering and dispatching, and a tiny number of unskilled workers. The total workforce needed after the scheme is implemented will almost certainly be less overall than previously, and although some new posts will be created it is mostly the unskilled and semi-skilled ones which will disappear.

Secondly, it is the case that in adulthood generally more skills will be needed for family and community life as well as for work. Children currently at school will need to leave with considerable reading competence, a sound grasp of number, good social and communication skills, and a proper knowledge of where to find information and how to act on it in our increasingly complex, technological and bureaucratic society. Those who do not have these skills may find themselves unemployment casualties, or unable to sustain a satisfying adult life.

Many jobs which used to require very few basic skills now require a great deal more. Some, for example, need a higher reading age than formerly. 'Reading age' is a rough and ready concept to describe competence in reading. If someone has a reading age of 10 it means he reads like the average ten-year-old. Thus a seven-year-old with a reading age of 10 would be well ahead of his fellows, a ten-year-old would be about average, and a school leaver with a reading age of 10 would be severely handicapped in adult life, unable to take in anything other than simple texts such as are used by primary school children. You need a reading age of about 15 or 16 to cope with this chapter. In other words average school leavers should be able to cope with it, even if they do not understand every word.

Shop stewards who used to negotiate orally now have to have a rudimentary knowledge of legislation covering matters such as unfair dismissals and safety at work. Much of the information about such Acts is written in quite complex language, and a shop steward with a very low reading age could not cope with the necessary reading, and would thus be unable to advise his colleagues appropriately.

A reading age of between 12 and 18 is required for various newspapers, and the mind-blowing complexity of some official forms is beyond the comprehension of most mortals, though this can be attributed to poor writing rather than to a defective human race. Similarly, although the mathematics of everyday life

97

SUGAR & GROWTH OF A MOULD

Follow these instructions.

1 Copy these two diagrams into your book.
   If your book is plain paper, lay a sheet of lined paper under the page.

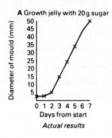 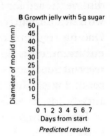

Answer these questions in sentences.

a Which experiment has most sugar in the growth jelly?

b Which of these three possibilities is the most likely? Give reasons for your answer.

1 Mould A and mould B will grow in the same way.
2 Mould A will grow faster than mould B.
3 Mould B will grow faster than mould A.

c Which of these graphs best fits your answer to question **b**? Copy it on the graph B drawn in your book.

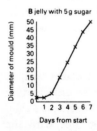 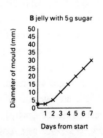 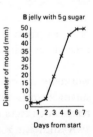

ASK YOUR TEACHER IF YOU SHOULD GO ON TO SHEET S5 OR E5

Figure 2 Pupils learn to find out for themselves: an experiment in growth (from *Science Watch*, P. Butler, D. Carrington, G. Ellis, Cambridge University Press, 1986).

can be simple and repetitive, some of it is not so straightforward. Many quite ordinary people fill in income tax forms, pay interest on loans, run a household budget, make VAT returns or have to calculate speed, distance and cost when undertaking a journey. In some fields of work, such as engineering, the mathematical demands are far beyond what they were in the past.

A further aspect of modern life is the speed and scale of knowledge gathering. A doctor, scientist, businessman or teacher curious about research in a particular field is often astonished to discover how many investigators have worked on the problem and written up their results in journals and books around the globe. One file of research in chemistry alone contains well over two million references, and computers must be used to search for relevant reports, the task now being beyond the human eye and hand. Every day thousands of further studies are added to these already vast repositories of information.

Teachers in school, therefore, realizing that the extent of our knowledge on almost every subject prevents them from communicating all of it to the next generation of children, have to spend some time on basic skills and knowledge and the rest on equipping their pupils with the ability to find and use relevant information (see, for example, Figure 2).

Yet another change in society which affects schools is the rapid development of technology. When hand-held calculators became available at reasonable prices, so that many children received them as presents and schools were able to contemplate purchasing sets of them, teachers faced a dilemma. Should they ignore the development and carry on as usual? Should they throw out most of their traditional numerical calculation work and just use calculators instead? Or should they give children an understanding of the relevant mathematics plus some practice in hand-worked solutions, and then show them how to use calculators to solve complex problems quickly and with understanding? Many teachers opted for the last solution.

A similar problem was faced when television appeared on a wide scale in almost every household. Some people saw it as a threat to human life, likely to produce a passive breed of spectator, and therefore not to be used in school, others felt it had exciting potential as an educational medium, capable of showing pupils a brilliantly performed Shakespeare play or an expensively produced film on volcanoes around the world such as no teacher could ever hope to make with limited resources.

Perhaps the most problematic aspect of all changes witnessed in our society in recent times is that it becomes increasingly difficult to predict what life will be like in the twenty-first century, when children currently in school will be adults, many playing key roles in their community. Some forecasters predict a life of endless leisure with the microprocessor revolution leading to automated factories, and a minute workforce.

Others guess that the revolution will not so much abolish work but rather lead to different kinds of jobs coming into existence. Just as people left the land to work in factories after the industrial revolution, so too they may leave factories to work in an enlarged leisure and recreational industry. As the factory machine became an extension of the human arm, so too the microprocessor might become an extension of the human brain, creating jobs and a life style we cannot accurately predict. If more people work in the leisure industry instead of factories then social skills would be most important, as no-one wants to find his leisure soured by people who cannot get on with their fellows (see Figure 3).

We may conclude, therefore, that schools have responded and must continue to respond to changes in society, whilst not always certain when and how change may come about. Increased demands for greater skill, for preparation, for community and family life and the world of work, for a quick response to technological innovation, for basic knowledge and strategies for finding further information, have led to several changes in primary and secondary schools, such as the Technical and Vocational Education Initiative (TVEI) for 14- to 18-year-olds, which placed more emphasis on the preparation of children for the world of work. It is to some of the questions about what and how we teach children in school that we now turn.

Primary schools

Primary education covers the 5–11 age range, and in some areas which have a first and middle school pattern, can include 12-year-olds. The 9–13 middle school is, for administrative purposes, regarded as a secondary school if most of its pupils are over 11.

Common arrangements of schools in the primary sector are shown below. Some schools have a nursery section for 3–5 year olds attached to them.

100

Talking Points

1 Discuss Wendy's physical appearance. Does physical appearance give any clues to the kind of person one is? Does physical appearance sometimes influence one's character and behaviour?

2 Wendy said she was fat and short, with freckles and pimples. Why didn't she describe herself in a kinder and more complimentary way? Why do young people often describe themselves in this way? How serious are they?

3 Wendy also tells us she was definitely the brightest girl in the class. Considering her behaviour when she received the invitation to the pool, do you agree?

4 What preparations do you and your friends make when you receive invitations?

Role-playing

Role-playing is similar to acting but less formal and with no written lines to speak. Instead, you try to become the person whose role you take over. Put yourself in his shoes—think and feel and talk and act as that person would.

You will find interesting situations developing between the role-players, often unexpected ones, and your own reactions in your new role may surprise you also.

Role-playing is frequently used by adults to help them understand themselves, and how and why crisis situations develop on the factory floor and in management. It is also used by groups of people who have to live and work together. It helps them to learn to recognise the crisis signals and how to take avoiding action before the danger point is reached.

You can deepen your own understanding of yourself and others if you take your roles seriously. You should also carefully watch others playing their roles.

1 Work in groups. Take Wendy's role, and those of her mother and younger members of her family who watch her preparations and tease her unmercifully. Mother tries to keep the peace . . .

2 Take the roles of Wendy's older brother and parents, and Wendy herself. He is preparing for his first date. Wendy and the younger members of the family tease him. He loses his temper. Mother pleads, but can't quieten him. Then Father comes in . . .

Figure 3 Learning oral and social skills: discussion and role-playing exercises (from *English for Living*, A. Rowe, Macmillan, London and Basingstoke, 1976).

1 Infant (5–7 year olds) followed by junior (7–11 year olds)
2 First (5–8 year olds) followed by middle (8–12 year olds)
3 First (5–9 year olds) followed by middle (9–13 year olds)

The idea of the primary school is that it lays the foundations for education by introducing children to important aspects of learning at a simple level, allowing this to be built upon at the secondary stage. Amongst the things to be learned will be important basic concepts in mathematics, science and humanities, and if all goes well there will be considerable development of children's language and ability to think.

In view of the shortness of children's attention at this age and the widely held view that they learn readily by doing something rather than being passive, there is usually some emphasis on so-called *activity methods*, which mean that children will be encouraged to discuss, explore and do, more frequently than look and listen. Thus those classrooms with rows of fixed desks, everyone facing the front and all doing the same task at the same time, so familiar in elementary schools earlier this century, have, in many schools, given way to small clusters of children seated around tables engaged in individual or group work.

Most primary schools are small, and this is reflected in the numbers of the various types of schools in England. There are about four times as many primary schools as secondary schools, and the latter are often much bigger and more complex in organization. Teachers usually take their own class for most of the day, whereas in secondary schools each subject may be taught by a different specialist. In recent years there has been some movement towards a degree of specialization in the primary school, and it is now more common for teachers to swap classes occasionally with another teacher so that each can give expert help to more than one group in Music, Art and Craft, number work, language or whatever happens to be his particular interest or specialism.

Buildings are of all shapes and sizes. Although most have been purpose-built over the last fifty years there are many older primary schools, some built well over 100 years ago, with solid walls, high windows and cramped classrooms. In more recent times school buildings have more window space, better lighting and ventilation, and are frequently flexible in design, allowing spaces to be used in different ways. There has been considerable use of transportable classrooms which can be set down temporarily in the grounds of a school with increasing numbers, and moved subsequently elsewhere if necessary. In some older schools the 'temporary' buildings erected fifty or sixty years ago still stand, apparently defying all attempts to have them demolished.

Open plan primary schools have few interior walls and can be used in a variety of ways. Many were built in the late 1960s and 1970s and were meant to suit the preferred style of teachers who found themselves spilling out into the corridors of traditional schools. Sometimes there are two or three large units within the school, each containing perhaps 100 or so pupils with three or four teachers. The teachers may work as a team or separately.

The open plan area will be divided up into various sections, subdivided perhaps by bookshelves, cupboards or sliding screens, one part carpeted, another with a vinyl floor covering, depending on the type of activity undertaken there. One area may have books, cassette recorders and headphones, to be used principally for reading and language work. Another part may contain maths books and equipment. A sink and formica topped surface may be found in another area, and children will don their aprons and paint, glue and make things there. There may be a 'quiet corner', a little ante-room where children can read on their own and for music or noisy activities there will probably be a sound-proofed conventional box classroom so no-one else will be disturbed.

A pupil working in such a school may start his project in the language area, move later to library and resources, go on to the 'messy area' to construct something, retire to the quiet corner for reflection and return to a table elsewhere to finish off. Teachers may be stationed in language or number areas, move freely around answering questions, checking progress and encouraging children, or work with a particular group of children in a certain topic in the more conventional one teacher/one class situation. There are many ways of working in open plan schools and teachers' views about such schools vary considerably, from enthusiastic support to great dislike. Similarly the buildings are different, some brilliant in design, others noisy and badly conceived.

Secondary schools

Before the second world war over 90 per cent of children aged 5–14 were educated in all-age elementary schools, and the idea of secondary education for all was a dream. After the war the common pattern was for children to be selected at the age of ten or eleven either for a grammar school or a secondary modern.

Provision varied according to the area in which children lived, and it was not unknown for 15 per cent of children to go to grammar schools in one area and 20 per cent in a nearby authority. Over the nation as a whole the range was wider still.

In certain parts of the country, notably London, there already existed comprehensive schools taking children of all abilities, and in 1965 the Labour government of the time issued a circular requesting local education authorities to submit plans for reorganizing secondary education in their area on comprehensive lines. Several schemes have been approved, and most local authorities opted to open some new schools and make the best use of existing buildings rather than underwrite the vast capital expenditure which would result from a total rebuilding programme.

Amongst schemes which were adopted were the following, in some cases in modified form.

1 All-through comprehensive (11–18-year-olds)
2 Junior comprehensive (11–14), senior comprehensive (14–18)
3 Junior comprehensive (11–16), senior comprehensive for those wishing to transfer at 13 and stay on after the minimum school-leaving age (13–18)
4 Junior comprehensive (11–16), sixth form or tertiary college (16+)
5 Middle school (9–13), senior comprehensive (13–18)

Consequently the 1970s saw considerable changes in secondary schools on a scale never experienced before. Not only did many schools reorganize, but at the same time the school-leaving age was raised to 16, there were increased problems of discipline, especially in inner-city areas, and schools often became bigger and more complex.

Since teachers now had to deal with the whole ability range in the same school many new books and curriculum packages were produced locally or nationally, and different forms of grouping were tried as they strove to find the fairest and most effective ways of teaching. Teachers who had never before taught the brightest pupils and those who had never previously worked with average and slow learners had to develop new professional skills to be able to teach across the whole ability range. Sadly, this period coincided with a spell of financial stringency, and most teachers, unable to obtain any release of time to study, plan and reflect, had to acquire these skills on the job.

Secondary school buildings are as different from one another as are primary school buildings. In many local authorities substantial secondary school building programmes have been undertaken during recent years. Some of these have been quite exciting multi-purpose buildings, having leisure centres, libraries, arts centres or a theatre attached to them, thus offering a superb set of facilities to the whole community. There are places where a stranger looking for the school is advised to follow the road signs marked 'Sports forum', and when he arrives he finds an unusual restriction forbidding street car parking during evenings and at weekends simply because the facilities are almost as widely used at those times as they are during the day.

During the 1980s many local authorities opted for a tertiary college form of reorganization for pupils between 16 and 19. The advantage was that wide choices could be offered, not only A levels but vocational awards such as those offered by the Business and Technician Educational Council (BTEC) or the City and Guilds of London Institute (CGLI). The disadvantage was that younger pupils in the 11–16 or 12–16 feeder secondary schools lost the benefit of having senior pupils in their school.

Teachers and teaching

There are well over 400,000 teachers in England and Wales, and currently people can train for teaching predominantly via two different routes. The first pattern is for 18-year-olds to spend three or four years at a university, polytechnic or college. During their course they study both specialized subjects and learn how to teach at the same time. This is called the *concurrent* pattern, and a student may be required to do teaching practice at any stage of his course. He will usually leave with a B.Ed. or B.A.(Ed.) degree.

The second pattern is for the would-be teacher to take his degree first at a university, polytechnic or college. Having obtained usually a B.A. or B.Sc. entirely devoted to the study of a single academic subject, such as French or Physics or some combination of academic subjects, but not containing any teaching practice or study of education, he will go on to spend a concentrated year devoted entirely to teacher training, at the end of which he obtains his licence to teach, the Postgraduate Certificate of Education. This is known as the *consecutive* pattern.

Until the 1970s it was generally the case that B.A. and B.Sc. graduates were trained entirely in universities, and non-graduates and B.Ed. graduates in colleges of education. Since then the situation has been much more fluid, and each pattern of training can be found in many different higher education situations, though some aspects of the previous system survive. Although the development of teacher training is difficult to predict, it looks as if in future all new teachers will be graduates possessing a B.A., B.Sc., or B.Ed. degree, and about half will come along the consecutive and half via the concurrent route. However, in 1989 the government introduced a licensed teacher scheme which allowed mature entrants with industrial or commercial experience to enter teaching with supervised on-the-job training. Governors may acquire some excellent recruits through this route, but it is crucial for proper training to be given, otherwise unsuitable people could create mayhem in the classroom.

There will be major problems recruiting sufficient teachers during the 1990s, when many retirements take place, and every effort will have to be made to widen the recruitment base, especially by attracting people who have good relevant experience.

It is important not to be misled by graduate status: many non-graduates are outstanding teachers who never had the opportunity to take a degree, and who would probably have been the stars of their B.Ed. or B.A./B.Sc. class had they had the opportunity. Indeed a large number of the most successful Open University graduates were formerly non-graduate teachers, and other teachers have gone on to take a degree from a university or college during their teaching career as mature, in-service students.

Once teachers have qualified there are several forms of in-service work they can undertake. During the 1980s there was a considerable shift to school-based courses for teachers. The teachers' contract allows for five days each year, known popularly as 'Baker days', after the minister who introduced them, when pupils are not in school but teachers are, which can be used for such purposes. Universities, polytechnics, colleges, local education authorities, teachers' centres, the DES, and a number of other bodies all provide courses of short or long duration.

Teachers can attend anything from one-hour sessions or half-day workshops up to a whole-week, one-term or one-year courses, the longer ones leading to further professional qualifications like advanced diplomas or Master's degrees. Release from school and secondment on salary have been difficult to obtain in recent years, and teachers are usually delighted to have governors' support for in-service training. Although many teachers have been frustrated by wishing to attend courses and not being able to, there is the equally important problem of the teacher who would benefit from in-service work but chooses not to take advantage of it.

The school-based or school-focused programme allows teachers to improvise something they feel is of use to their community and draw in outsiders as necessary. There are several examples of governors attending parts or the whole of such courses and finding the experience extremely valuable. A typical programme for a one-day, school-based in-service course, using a mixture of home talent and visiting speakers, is shown on p. 109.

Teaching is a very busy job. Some studies of teachers have shown that they engage in as many as 1000 contacts with children in a day, when they ask or are asked questions, praise or reprimand, assign tasks, or respond to demands on their attention. This busy professional life style can extend over the whole year, making 5000 such contacts a week and several millions in a whole career. Put another way, imagine tapping your pet tortoise on its shell every four seconds, the effect on its nervous system would be considerable, the RSPCA would soon pay you a call, and no doubt the tortoise would be pressing its local authority for secondment elsewhere or for some shell-based in-service work.

In addition, teachers nowadays fill many roles. In some schools they even find themselves acting as front-line social workers, the first to see a bruised child or hear a family hard-luck story. Below are but some of the roles which teachers may find themselves filling at some time during a busy professional week.

Expert	Helping children learn information, or knowing where to find it in various subject areas, answering children's questions.
Counsellor	Advising pupils about careers, personal problems, important decisions.
Social worker	Dealing with problem families, children from broken homes, liaising with various social services.

Parent	Acting as substitute mother or father.
Jailer	Coping with pupils who would rather not be at school, dealing with truants.
Bureaucrat	Filling in registers, forms, returns or orders.
Public relations officer	Explaining to parents what the school is doing, dealing with local radio and newspapers.
Assessor	Marking books, grading tests, devising and administering examinations, writing references.
Technician	Assembling or dismantling equipment.
Manager	Making decisions about the most effective use of available resources.

It is because teaching is an exacting job and because most teachers are professional and committed to their work that the occasional teacher who is incompetent becomes conspicuous.

The 1986 Education Act introduced the whole question of teacher appraisal, which is now required by law, though it is left to LEAs to decide how it should be done. There are many ways of appraising teachers and most teachers themselves like to place the emphasis on helping teachers improve their professional skills, rather than merely giving them a mark out of ten.

Any parent will confirm that children who like their teachers skip happily to school, and those who do not have to be cajoled into attending. Teachers themselves are very embarrassed to find as a colleague one of the small number of ill-suited or inept practitioners, and, contrary to popular belief, teachers do not have a licence to teach for life, come what may. Amongst the more thorny problems which occasionally surface at governors' meetings will be found that of the teacher about whom there are serious complaints.

There is not, in England and Wales, a teaching council and a professional code of conduct which, if broken, leads to teachers being 'struck off the list' or disbarred in quite the same way as happens in the medical and legal professions. On the other hand the procedure is not radically different. If a teacher commits a criminal offence or is guilty of serious misconduct he will undoubtedly be asked to appear before the local authority's disciplinary committee or its equivalent, and he may lose his job. Furthermore, the Home Office reports all serious convictions of teachers to the Secretary of State who, after giving the teacher an

RESOURCES FOR LEARNING

9.00   *Introduction: recent developments in resource-based learning*
       Mr J. Brown, Senior Adviser, Exchester

9.45   *Adapting and extending the traditional school library*
       Mrs A. Johnson, Head of Exchester West Comprehensive School

10.30   Coffee

10.45   Discussion in departmental groups of implications for various subjects

12.00   Plenary session

12.30   Lunch

1.30   *How children learn from various media*
       Dr C. Smith, Dept. of Education, Exchester University

2.15   Practical sessions, each member of staff to join one group

A. Making tape-slide sets	Dr Smith
B. Micro-computer software	Mrs Johnson
C. Assembling sets of newspaper cuttings and archive	Mrs B. Phillips (Head of History)
D. Making and using television material	Mrs L. Thomas (Head of Biology)
E. The interactive videodisc – the BBC Domesday Project	Mrs D. Naylor (Head of Media Studies) Exchester South Comprehensive School

3.45   Plenary session

A typical programme for a one-day, school-based in-service course.

opportunity to make representations, may order that that person be no longer employed as a teacher. (Car parking offences are not reported!) Such blacklisted teachers may not be employed elsewhere without having been reinstated by the DES. [The blacklist is officially known as 'List 99'.]

The incompetent rather than criminal teacher is a different matter, though he too is liable to dismissal. Usually heads of department and heads of schools aided by LEA advisers and HMI will make exhaustive attempts to help someone in this position. If, however, people are satisfied that all help has failed or been rejected then, provided proper warnings have been issued and proper channels gone through, this teacher too can lose his job. What has been said above applies equally to heads. The reason that a certain popular belief persists that the teachers or heads cannot be shown the door is that the process is rightly long-winded and is not undertaken lightly. Certainly in any school which has a dismissal case the governors will find it figures high and frequently on their agenda.

We have spent some time on the question of incompetent or malevolent teachers only because when they are encountered they cause the greatest distress to their pupils, their colleagues and the authorities. It must be stressed, however, that this is a small, if problematic, section of a huge community, most of whom are highly professional and dedicated to their job.

Curriculum

The knowledge explosion and changes in society have put immense pressure on the curriculum. Consider these short extracts from history and geography textbooks written in the 1870s when pupils had to learn off by heart a set of packaged answers and repeat these like a catechism. They reflect the society of their day, when an uneducated peasantry received its first compulsory education at the hands of untrained teachers handling large classes. Life in family and society was stern, children were to be seen and not heard, and unquestioning obedience was encouraged and valued.

Q Who was Henry VIII?
A Son of Henry VII

Q What was his character?
A As a young man, he was bluff, generous, right royal, and very handsome

Q How was he when he grew older?
A He was bloated, vain, cruel and selfish.

110

Q What is the climate of England?
A Moist, but healthy

Q What is the character of the English people?
A Brave, intelligent and very persevering.

Q What is the size of England?
A About 430 miles long and 320 broad.

In the last 100 years children have been encouraged to assume a less subservient role, a great deal has been discovered about how people learn and fail to learn, and it is likely that the style of much of what is taught in the curriculum in modern schools is to offer pupils more opportunity for individual thought than did old textbooks. On the other hand one will still see mechanical and senseless rote learning at all levels, and some critics feel there has been too little movement away from authoritarian teacher-directed learning.

The National Curriculum

For most of this century England and Wales were unique in Europe in leaving individual schools to fashion their own curriculum. The 1988 Education Act established a National Curriculum, something common in mainland Europe.

The National Curriculum consists of religious education and *core subjects*: mathematics, English and science (plus Welsh in Welsh-speaking schools); and *foundation subjects*: (a) history, geography, technology, music, art and physical education (plus Welsh in non-Welsh speaking schools), (b) a modern foreign language (secondary pupils only).

Two national councils, a National Curriculum Council (NCC) and a School Examinations and Assessment Council (SEAC) were set up following the 1988 Act. The NCC receives reports from special subject councils which advise on attainment targets for children of different ages in fields like mathematics and science. The SEAC oversees arrangements for testing pupils at the key ages of 7, 11, 14 and 16, as required by the 1988 Act, to see how well they have met the attainment targets.

Test results will be made available to governors, the LEA and parents, as mentioned in Chapter 2, and governors must keep these under review. There is some latitude within the National Curriculum itself, because the government, although it has prescribed the subjects, does not specify how these should be taught. Heads, teachers and governors should, therefore, still be able to create some flexibility with a little imagination. Nor is it essential for every aspect of the National Curriculum to be taught within a discrete subject heading. Technology, for example, will occur in more than one field, and the well-established traditions of project and topic work in primary schools, described below, allow for subjects such as geography and history to be taught under themes like 'canals' or 'our village'.

There has been some concern that national tests, especially for 7-year-olds, produce a high level of anxiety, and it is up to governors to monitor this by keeping in touch with parents. National tests should, in any case, only be a part of a school's assessment programme. Many teachers make regular use of short tests and the national tests every four years or so ought not to be allowed to dominate what is taught in school.

One matter certain to be of interest to governors is the publication of schools' test scores in an authority or region in 'league table' form. Crude comparisons tell us little about the quality of teaching in a school. For example, a school in a socially deprived area is likely to score below a school in a socially privileged part of town, but not because the teaching is poor, rather because the school's intake is of lower intellectual ability. If Liverpool Football Club played the Little Piddlington Cubs at football and won by eight goals to nil that could actually represent a triumph for the Cubs and a poor display for the professionals. League tables of schools' exam scores must be treated with the same degree of caution and background factors taken into account, otherwise much unjustified misery, or complacency, will ensue.

Primary school curriculum

Primary schools operate various patterns. Some follow a timetable of thirty- or forty-minute lessons, sometimes with the 'basics' in the morning and art, craft, music and project work in the afternoon. Others have what is known as the *integrated day*, which may be based on no formal timetable of subjects at all but allow teachers and pupils to spend the day on a variety of individual and group work. Teachers who operate the integrated approach successfully have to prepare skilfully, and record progress meticulously. Usually each child has a certain set of assignments

112

	Number	Daily Diary	Project (personal)	Project (class)	Art/Craft	Reading	Comment
Mary	✓	✓	✓		✓	✓	Now understands fractions very well.
John	✓	✓		✓		✓	Moved to red readers but found it hard going.
Colin	✓	✓	✓	✓		✓	
Alice	✓	✓		✓		✓	Beginning to lose interest in water project, must switch tomorrow.

he must complete, some mathematics, some reading, some written work, and then a topic, often of his own choosing. At its best the system allows a child to pursue each task in his own time and not have to break off at some inappropriate point.

Well organized primary classrooms are a joy to see, there being an air of busy enjoyment around the place. Badly organized classrooms have children wasting time, spending days over unexacting tasks, and learning little.

A typical daily record of four children from a class taught along integrated lines might look as shown on p. 113, a tick denoting that the teacher had checked progress in the area.

Reading

There are hundreds of well produced reading books suitable for children, some graded for beginners, others beautifully illustrated and in appropriate language for children who have learned to read a little and need to become more proficient through enjoying reading.

Several methods of teaching reading have been in and out of vogue in recent years:

(a) *Phonics* is the best-known traditional method, and involves the pupil in learning to recognize the individual letters and sounds and then blend them into the whole word: d – o – g equals dog. It is more confusing when words like bough, cough, through and iron are encountered, but some books use entirely words which are phonically 'true' and do not confuse the learning in the early stages (see Figure 4).

(b) *Look and say/whole word* is a method whereby pupils learn the whole word as a shape or pattern. The teacher often uses pictures and flashcards at the outset, so that a child might learn to recognize even a complex word like 'television' quite early on. The advantage of this method is that reading matter can be made more interesting, involving sentences like 'John liked watching television' rather than 'The cat sat on the mat'. One disadvantage is that children sometimes fail to distinguish accurately the components of longer words and see, for example, 'television' as tel- followed by a jumble of letters. They might therefore read 'telephone', 'telegram' or even

114

The Trip

When Pat and I went down to Skegness on a bus trip, it was too hot for us to dig in the sands for long, so we went for a swim. After this, I had the bad luck to cut my hand on a bit of glass that had been left on the sands.

Figure 4 Extract from a phonic reader for six-year-olds (*Royal Road Reader*, Book 1, Grafton Books, 1970).

'telxyzzzon' as 'television'. Thus many teachers prefer to use some combination of whole word reading and phonics in their teaching of reading.

(c) *Sentence/language experience* A more recent method tries to integrate reading and writing rather than teach them separately. For example, the 'Breakthrough to Literacy' project (see Figure 5 opposite) provides children with a simple aid to sentence writing. Some 200 or so high frequency words are already printed on separate plastic strips and the child can add words of his own on blanks. Children can write their own sentences by assembling a mixture of printed words and their own choices in the Sentence Maker.

Few teachers adhere rigidly to one mode of teaching reading, and most will exploit some combination of methods and use both carefully graded reading schemes, which take children from beginner to fluent reader, alongside suitable children's fiction and books of general interest.

What is often neglected, however, is some work on the higher skills of reading. Once a child can read with a fair degree of confidence he needs to learn the kind of reading skills essential in much of adolescent and adult life. These skills involve the ability to scan or skim, read rapidly, to slow down and read over again a difficult passage, to use a book index or library catalogue, to make notes summarizing sections or recording key points, to discriminate between styles of writing, and to recognize fact from opinion. Some researcher colleagues of ours once studied children in school libraries by taking photographs every few seconds. The only person who ever went near the catalogue section was the librarian lovingly inserting more cards for the children not to consult.

Writing

Before the typewriter, having a 'fair hand' was an important selling point in the job market and a valued attribute in Victorian society, when clerks painstakingly entered pages of beautifully scripted entries into huge leatherbound ledgers. Today although good handwriting is still cultivated in most schools, there is also considerable attention devoted to what children write as well as how they write it. Teaching young children how to write involves their learning in the first instance how to hold the pen or pencil, form letters and write from left to right. They are usually taught the small letters first and capitals later, and normally learn to

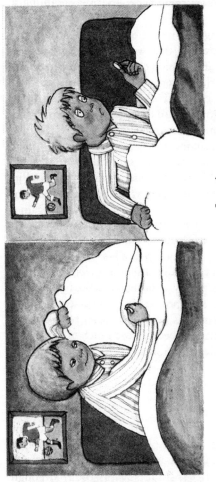

When I went to bed
I put it under my pillow.

12

In the morning
my tooth had gone.
There was some money
under my pillow.

13

Figure 5 Extract from one of the Breakthrough Books, part of the Breakthrough to Literacy project, which enables children to read and write sentences using word cards taken from their own Sentence Maker folders. (*The Loose Tooth*, David Mackay *et al.*, Schools Council/Longman, 1970).

117

print first using simple traditional letter forms or one of the italic styles.

We use writing in many contexts and for many purposes in our ordinary lives, so children will learn to write for different audiences. Once having mastered the act of writing they will write stories, accounts of their experiences and reports of work undertaken.

The term 'creative writing' has been frequently used in recent years. For some it represented all that was best in the so-called primary school revolution, after which children were encouraged to express themselves in their own way rather than ape the writings and views of their elders. To the critics it was a sloppy 'anything goes' notion likely to be full of wrong spellings ignored by the teacher afraid to dampen emergent genius.

As ever the reality was that few teachers conformed to either stereotype. Most sought to achieve some spontaneity from their pupils, and corrected spellings and punctuation judiciously, neither condoning errors nor fuming with rage at a missing apostrophe.

Analysis of a primary school child's day might show him writing a diary entry, a letter, a note to a friend, an account of a school trip, a made-up story, copying from a book or blackboard, describing the weather, and compiling a shopping list, all during the one period of 24 hours. Many children in school will write more and for a wider range of purposes than their parents. When the quality of children's writing is poor it is either because they have been given little practice, or because too much of what they write is mechanically copied from books, the blackboard or worksheets.

Mathematics

There is a great deal of talk about 'old' and 'new' mathematics, which often annoys mathematicians, who find nothing 'new' about so-called new maths. It has always been there, they argue, it simply was not being taught in most schools.

Recent primary school mathematics teaching has tried to get away from mechanical learning and endless repetition, and move towards letting children understand the mathematics they learn. Children will learn not simply that $5 \times 4 = 20$, but that 5×4 is also the same as 4×5 or 10×2 or $5 + 5 + 5 + 5$ or (3×5)

118

+ 5. They will learn about shapes and get the feel of their properties by making and extending various shapes, rotating or classifying them. They will also learn the measurement of time, length and mass (see Figures 6 and 7, pp. 120 and 121).

APPLIED MATHS

In general they will learn better at primary age by directly experiencing mathematics, so that much of the work will be practical using blocks, counters and other equipment as necessary, or involving children in considering aspects of their immediate environment, like measuring the volume of their classroom, the height of their friends, or what they can do in a minute, or finding circle and triangle shapes encountered in everyday life.

Some of the debate about primary school mathematics centres around the teaching of tables, and adults often fantasize that they were themselves mathematical wizards at an early age because they can still chant a nine times table. Critics of primary maths teaching complain that some pupils have to work out 9 × 8 by writing out the number 8 nine times and adding it all up. Skilful primary school teachers recognize that both an intuitive understanding of mathematics and, on occasion, a speedy and accurate response are required, and prepare for children for several

Can you hold your breath for one minute?
Ask your friend to time you with a stop-watch.

What else can you do in one minute?
Ask your friend to time you.

I can count to ☐

I can breathe ☐ times.

I can write ☐ numerals.

I can read ☐ words.

I can draw ☐ squares.

I can jump ☐ times.

I can walk ☐ steps.

Measurement: the minute   47

Figure 6   An extract from *Mathematics for Schools*, Level 1, Book 6 – for five- to seven-year-olds (Harold Fletcher *et al.*, Addison-Wesley, 1970).

eventualities, without either boring them to death with mindless repetition or failing to drive it all home after the experience and discovery phase.

Science

A primary school survey by the DES in 1978 was very critical of the science teaching which HM Inspectors saw. Some children appeared to be learning nothing at all about science until they reached secondary school, and only a small number of teachers appeared to be doing worthwhile and exciting work. Yet children at primary school age are immensely curious about their surroundings, and it is a great pity that few teachers preparing to

120

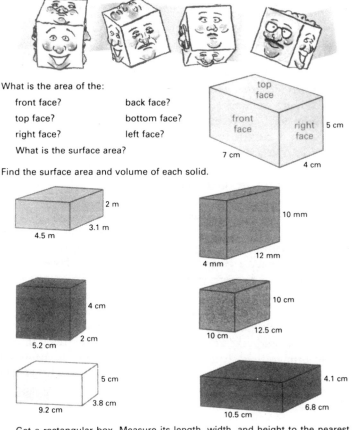

What is the area of the:

front face?	back face?
top face?	bottom face?
right face?	left face?

What is the surface area?

Find the surface area and volume of each solid.

Get a rectangular box. Measure its length, width, and height to the nearest centimetre.
Calculate its surface area and volume.

Determine the surface area and volume of your classroom.

43

Figure 7 A page from *Ginn Mathematics*, Level 7, Textbook 2, for older primary pupils (Ginn, 1985).

121

teach the under-11s had any significant science course in their training until recent times.

A great deal of science can be learned from the immediate environment, and children of 3 or 4 often ask important scientific questions. Below are just seven of the thousands of questions children ask their teachers or parents which can lead on to simple work in science or technology:

1 Why do germs make you ill?
2 Why do things fall when you drop them?
3 Where do birds go in winter?
4 Why do we need oil?
5 Why am I out of breath when I run fast?
6 What is electricity and why can it kill you?
7 How does a calculator do sums so quickly?

Skilful teachers use every opportunity to engage children's interest in science. Many toys can be used to investigate basic scientific principles, for example how high a ball bounces on wood, carpet, polystyrene or water. The working of the human body is of concern to children and early health education can deal with tooth decay, a balanced diet or pollution. Elastic bands, lollipop sticks and construction toys can be useful for elementary education in technology.

It is vital for all adults to show an interest in and be knowledgeable about science and technology, and primary school governors should take an interest in what is being done in this area of primary school life as well as the three Rs. It should be remembered, however, that although some primary schools may set aside time for science on a timetable, others may choose to teach science as part of an integrated approach via project work.

Secondary school curriculum

The secondary school curriculum is too vast to describe in a short space, and much of what has been said about primary schools above applies to the secondary sector.

In some schools brand new subjects have appeared which may not be familiar to parents' and grandparents' generation, or they may be contemporary versions of lessons formerly under a different name. For example, in New York drugs education had

29a Experiment
Looking for a law

Take a seesaw and balance it on the wedge at the centre. Put some loads on each side. You should put the loads at the marks so that you know when a load is one step out or two steps out or four steps out from the centre. Don't put a load $2\frac{3}{4}$ steps out because that would make it harder to find out the scientific story of seesaws. First make the seesaw balance with two piles of loads (pennies), one each side.

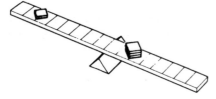

When you have it balanced, the seesaw will tip over to one side and stay there, and it will tip over to the other side and stay there. You will not be able to make it stay exactly balanced in mid-air. That is because it is sitting on top of the support at the centre, ready to fall over either way. But this will be just like 'weighing sweets': when the scales are exactly balanced and you find ever so little more would tip the scale one way or the other.

You have balanced the seesaw with two piles of pennies. *How can you move the pennies and keep the balance?*

Find out what you can about a balancing seesaw, with different loads on it. Make notes in your notebook of what happens. See if you can find out some rule or story that you could tell other people about balancing loads.

29b Experiment
Using your law

Use a large seesaw made from a plank balanced on a brick, and your knowledge of the 'lever law' to weigh your partner.

Figure 8 Children learn to look for and apply a law in Physics (from *Nuffield Physics*, Year 1, Longman, 1978).

to become a major concern at both elementary and high school level, because so many children were dying from using heroin or one of the lethal drugs, or were seriously injuring their health, and parents themselves, never having been taught at school about the effects of various drugs, were clamouring for informed advice to be given to children in good time. In a different context a course called 'integrated craft' might contain some recognizable elements from traditional woodwork and metalwork lessons, but might also deal with leather, ceramics, plastics and textiles, and involve the use of modern power-tools and machinery, as well as traditional craftsmanship.

It would take several books to describe all that is happening in secondary schools, so a brief description of certain developments will suffice. As in primary school teaching there has been emphasis in certain secondary school science curricula on discovery learning. Great scientists devise theories which they then put to the test. If successive carefully controlled experiments produce the same findings the theory is upheld. Thus pupils may speculate about what will happen if a current from batteries is passed through several bulbs. Various experiments will be conducted by groups to test out their 'hypotheses'. Finally a principle will be extracted from the results and compared with the textbook versions of scientific laws (see, for example, Figure 8).

In foreign language teaching there has been some movement towards stressing oral competence. Instead of the turgid grammar-bound books of yesteryear based on the traditions of Latin teaching, a modern language teacher today may choose from a vast selection of books, flashcards, filmstrips, tapes and audio-visual courses which make use of sound tapes of native speakers and pictures of scenes in the country whose language is being studied. Some schools have had language laboratories installed which offer each pupil a booth containing a tape recorder, whilst the teacher sits at a console and is able to monitor individuals or talk to the whole class. Many courses currently on the market stress everyday life in the country being studied, and children learn the conversation necessary for shopping, travel, family life and leisure (see Figure 9).

English teaching in secondary schools has become very broad, and English teachers may find themselves doing a wide range of children's fiction and adult literature, creative writing, drama, developing oral skills and self-confidence and a host of other assignments. The Bullock Report *A Language for Life* in 1975

124

C'EST EXTRA

Task 1

How would you ask for the following?

1 a some bananas
  b a kilo of bananas

2 a some ham
  b 5 slices of ham

3 a some mineral water
  b a bottle of mineral water

4 a some cake
  b 3 pieces of cake

5 a some chips
  b a portion of chips

6 a some crisps
  b a bag of crisps

Task 2

Les paniers de provisions

A. Make a list of what's in this basket.

B. Answer these questions about what's in the second basket.

Example

1. Non, il n'y a pas de vin.
2. Oui, il y a deux bouteilles de limonade.

1. Est-ce qu'il y a du vin?
2. Est-ce qu'il y a de la limonade?
3. Est-ce qu'il y a des biscuits?
4. Est-ce qu'il y a du jambon?
5. Est-ce qu'il y a des chips?
6. Est-ce qu'il y a du fromage?
7. Est-ce qu'il y a du pain?
8. Est-ce qu'il y a des sardines?
9. Est-ce qu'il y a du saucisson?
10. Est-ce qu'il y a du pâté?

C. Now imagine that you are preparing food for a picnic. Describe what you would put in your basket.

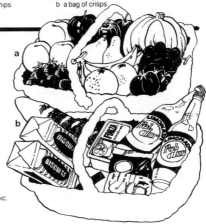

Figure 9   An extract from *Tricolore* 1B (from *Tricolore*, Stage One, Pupil's Book 1B, Sylvia Honnor, Ron Holt and Heather Mascie-Taylor, E.J. Arnold, 1980).

stressed that every teacher was responsible for teaching language, on the grounds that it was better for a Physics or Maths teacher to explain what 'inversely proportional' meant when it occurred in a lesson, rather than to opt out, claiming that the English teacher would have to deal with it one day. Nevertheless a great deal of responsibility for language development still does fall on the shoulders of English teachers.

For several years there had been a tendency for some English teachers to react vigorously against language work, partly because of the tedious emphasis on clause analysis, punctuation and spelling, which had made English lessons unpopular in many secondary schools. Since the Bullock Report time spent on language has tended to increase. More English teachers will now try to teach the higher skills of reading and will attempt to sensitize children to the effects of various language choices. For example, a class may study several letters sent to a person, some pompous, some long-winded, some flippant, some insulting, and discover how words are used to convey messages and what impact they have on the recipient (see, for example, Figure 10). Similarly they may study different accounts of the same political, social or sporting occasion in a number of newspapers to see how writers of various persuasions describe the same events.

Figure 10 Children learn the importance of emphasis and voice intonation in communication (from *Your Language. Two*, Maura Healy, Macmillan, London and Basingstoke, 1981).

126

Other subjects too have seen changes or pressure for more to be included in their syllabus. Pupils studying History or Geography may do their own survey work, consulting archives, old newspapers, interviewing local farmers or shopkeepers, going on field trips to see industrial archaeology or geographical features. Local history and geography may figure prominently in the early stages of secondary schools, and urban geography – the study of housing, roadways, the location of precincts, factories and supermarkets, has become a legitimate part of some pupils' lessons.

Religious education has often been widened in multiracial schools to include a comparative study of other religious beliefs, or sometimes to include moral education in an attempt to equip

Type of programme	Viewing times. p.m.							
	4/5	5/6	6/7	7/8	8/9	9/10	10/11	11/12
News and talks on current affairs								
Talks on other serious subjects								
Documentaries								
Serious music								
Lighter music								
Pop music								
Opera and ballet								
Serious plays								
Comedy and music-hall								
Serials								
Old films								
Religious services								
Sport								
Quiz and panel games								
Children's programmes								

Figure 11 Studying media: children analyse and discuss their television viewing habits, using the above documentation as a starting point (from *Life in Our Society*, vol. 2, K. Lambert, Nelson, 1975).

children with a sense of right and wrong. For other teachers religious education remains exclusively the study of Christianity. Some forms of RE syllabus have been very wide indeed, including several world religions and even permitting reference to communism, always guaranteed to provoke a burst of letters when announced in the press.

In addition to what might be called the traditional secondary school subjects there are several hybrids or new areas, some of which are described below:

Humanities/Social Studies

Often this combines geography, history and perhaps another subject. Pupils may study a theme like 'transport', 'housing', 'man in society', 'machines and our lives' with reference to our own and other societies, including primitive tribes. Although several commercially produced courses exist many teachers have worked together to improvise their own.

Media studies

Children will spend hours of their lives watching television, yet until recently almost nothing was done in school to encourage discrimination. Television in particular, radio and newspapers to a lesser degree, inform and shape children's attitudes to a variety of issues, offer heroes and villains and influence their money spending and leisure habits. A media studies course might involve pupils in learning how to make television and radio programmes, understanding how news programmes or newspapers are put together, learning the tricks used by advertisers and politicians to persuade buyers or voters, analysing popular entertainment shows, and seeing how important mass media are in our daily lives (see, for example, Figure 11).

Political education

The 1986 Education Act ruled out political indoctrination, not that much of that actually occurred. Most people advocating some systematic teaching about politics do not indoctrinate but rather look at politics as the use of power in any society including our own. Thus how decisions are made locally, nationally or internationally is of central interest, and party politics is but one part of this concern. In a true democracy, it is argued, adults must understand the decision-making process. Rather than listen to tedious lectures about Parliament or what rates are used for, pupils may well simulate some local problem, where to build a shopping centre or a motorway, and role play the various parties involved as money is raised, plans devised, votes cast and objections heard. Pupil observers are receiving political education by attending governors' meetings.

Personal, social and moral education (PSME)

In some schools departments called 'Personal relationships' have been established and PSME is built into the timetable. In others it is not formally scheduled and taught, but is part of what is sometimes called the 'hidden curriculum', a phrase devised to describe the many things schools teach and children learn which are not officially on the timetable of lessons. For example, if one feels a sense of lurking violence on the premises of a particular school, the building is vandalized, pupils barged out of the way along corridors, wall displays tatty, crumbling and defaced and no-one apparently cares, there seems to be a powerful message that human beings do not count, that disorder is acceptable and that concern for others is not to be encouraged. If on the other hand, the school clearly is concerned about the welfare of its members, that children are not bullied, that those of modest ability are not scoffed at, that privacy can be respected or that a craftsman's pride in collective achievement is permissible, then important social education is taking place every time an insensitive pupil is counselled.

Health education

Doctors tell us that adults are often astonishingly ill-informed about the workings of their own body, pregnant mothers unaware that smoking may cause smaller babies, and worse, obese middle-aged men ignorant of the consequences of lack of exercise, drinkers not knowledgeable about the effects on the body's vital organs of

129

excessive alcohol, and people on high dosages of amphetamines or barbiturates apparently not realizing they have a problem. Some interesting work on all aspects of health education is being undertaken in many schools nowadays, and whilst information alone will not necessarily prevent abuse of the human body, it may help in those cases where people might unwittingly do themselves a mischief through their own ignorance.

Technical and vocational education initiative (TVEI)

In response to the concerns about school leavers who were not prepared for the world of work, the Training Agency (or Manpower Services Commission (MSC) as it then was) sponsored experimental schemes in technical and vocational education for 14- to 18-year-olds throughout the 1980s. Pupils studied and acquired work experience in various fields, such as microtechnology, the caring professions (e.g. nursing and social work), the built environment (jobs in the building trade), to help them understand the range of jobs they might one day do and appreciate which qualities they would need to develop. (An example of a project from a technology course is given in Figure 12.)

After initial pilot experiments the scheme spread to most schools. The emphasis was on learning by direct experience, and pupils were encouraged to negotiate much more for themselves than had previously been the case. Many pupils took formal qualifications as part of their course, and some obtained the Certificate in Prevocational Education (CPVE) at the age of 17 or so.

Postscript

We have several times apologized for the inadequacy of the brief description of some of the recent developments which affect life in school. Inevitably any attempt to encapsulate the vast complexity of what happens in the lessons of over 400,000 teachers in a single chapter must omit a great deal. It would also be wrong to pretend that all the recent developments described above take place in our schools. There are schools which have never changed for years, others which have seen innovation without change (i.e. the introduction of some new curriculum

The bridge was already known as 'Galloping Gertie' because of vertical oscillations that were set up in the central deck section, even with fairly light winds. There was also a tendency to twist about an axis running along the length of the bridge. The bridge was able to withstand the vertical oscillations, but a combination of the two types caused by a wind which had a speed of less than 20 m s proved fatal.

Make the model bridge shown in Fig. 10.2a. Place the clamp stands about 500 mm apart, use thread for the suspension cable and hinges, and a 700 mm by 100 mm piece of thin cardboard for the deck. You can see the vertical oscillations that were set up in the Tacoma Bridge by moving the deck at point *A* up and down vertically (Fig. 10.2b). These are called flexural oscillations. Where does the deck appear to remain stationary?

Now, by twisting the deck at point *B* from side to side, you can see the so-called torsional oscillations. With a partner at *A* and you at *B*, you can see how the catastrophic oscillations developed in the Tacoma Bridge. Figure 10.3 shows this diagrammatically.

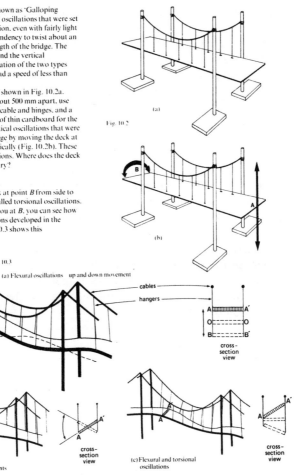

Fig. 10.2

Fig. 10.3

(a) Flexural oscillations — up and down movement

cables
hangers

cross-section view

(b) Torsional oscillations — sideways twisting movements

cross-section view

(c) Flexural and torsional oscillations

cross-section view

Figure 12   Pupils study the stresses on a suspension bridge as part of a Schools Council modular technology course (*Problem Solving Workbook*, from Oliver and Boyd in association with the National Centre for School Technology, 1986).

131

package but with the same strategies used beforehand) and schools dizzy with the whirligig of new courses, changes in organization and personnel and baffled by their own complexity and fluidity.

Nor would it be correct to say that new ideas invariably ensure outstanding success. We have both in our travels round schools seen brand new audio-visual language courses where the children senselessly and uncomprehendingly chanted German phrases over and over again like reluctant conscripts to some junior Nuremburg rally.

Nevertheless despite some poor schools and inadequate teachers it is our view that the majority of teachers in both primary and secondary schools have spent a great deal of time and effort attempting to improve children's education in school with considerable success. It will repay conscientious governors handsomely to become as well-informed as they possibly can about what is happening in schools today.

In particular, as the National Curriculum is introduced step by step over the years following the 1988 Education Act, governors should make every effort to study the various attainment targets for children at different stages of their education, and to look at the new books and teaching materials used by teachers implementing the National Curriculum.

In the following chapter we shall look at some of the issues faced in schools and frequently reported in the press and on television or radio.

6

Issues in education

The relationship between professionals and interested but lay parties in education is in some respects analogous to that obtaining in the medical profession. It would be a bold patient who would instruct the surgeon where to make the incision, but on the other hand he is probably entitled to know whether surgery is the only solution, when he is to be operated on, and to be listened to when describing his symptoms, apprehension or curiosity.

Many of the major issues in education are always with us. What and how shall we teach children? Are we preparing them adequately for adult life? What sort of examination system do we need? Are parents sufficiently well informed about their children's progress? Sometimes, however, it is difficult for governors to join in or even understand the discussion because it may be couched in unfamiliar language.

We are not referring here to the needlessly complex jargon occasionally introduced to make simple issues cloudy by inventing pretentious phrases such as 'learning stimulus materials' (toys), 'materially disadvantaged' (poor), 'endemic reduced placement opportunities' (unemployment) or 'informal decision-making sub-unit' (staffroom bridge four). It is rather that certain changes in the educational system occur suddenly, bringing with them new organizations or terminology sometimes simple in language but difficult to grasp unless one knows the background.

Thus phrases like, 'The GCSE 10 per cent coursework option has increased the load on the English staff'; 'We need to make active tutorial work a more central part of our pastoral care system'; or 'The lower school staff are trying out diagnostic tests and profiling this year' are all simple to explain, but might not be fully understood in the first instance.

In this chapter we shall take a number of issues regularly discussed by people connected with schools and sketch a little of the relevant background.

Pastoral care

Looking after the welfare of children has always been a central part of the teacher's job, especially with young children, and the phrase 'pastoral care' is commonly used.

In large schools, where children might easily be lost in the crowd if proper steps were not taken, there is often considerable planning put into looking after children's welfare. Usually the school is broken up into smaller units such as upper, middle and lower school, year groups or houses, and one of the deputy heads may be given special responsibility for pastoral care.

In some schools children have a personal tutor who, if possible, stays with them through more than one year of their career. In others there may be one or more counsellors who spend much of their time advising children about their personal problems, their career or their schoolwork. Increasingly, time is scheduled specially for tutor groups to spend with the teacher assigned to look after their welfare. Some teachers draw up an elaborate programme of activities for their class so that matters of concern can be discussed. Sometimes this becomes a central part of the school's personal, social and moral development scheme.

The British tradition of counselling is different from the American style. In many American high schools there is a strong and powerful counselling department whose head has deputy principal status. Sometimes there is conflict between the subject teachers and the counsellors about who should advise the pupil on careers or university entrance. On the other hand, where the American system works well the pupil has a superb professional service given by trained and caring experts. In Britain there tends to be either no counsellor at all, all teachers being expected to include counselling as part of their repertoire of professional skills, or a single counsellor who works closely with teachers.

The one teacher/one class system in most primary schools allows the class teacher to take full responsibility for each child's schooling and personal welfare. The smallness of a school does not by itself, however, guarantee sound pastoral care, though it is usually there in a natural unpretentious and unsculptured way. Parents usually receive strong messages from their children that teachers either are or are not interested in their welfare.

One problem sometimes arises over records. Schools which pride themselves on good pastoral care may either encourage teachers to keep everything in their heads or to make a detailed record. If, for example, a child has been beaten by a drunken parent and a teacher discovers this he may keep the knowledge to himself. If he leaves, however, a new teacher may not understand why the child is timid and withdrawn. On the other hand if the first teacher, in an attempt to help his colleagues understand the child better, enters a short comment on the pupil's confidential record card, he runs the risk of being accused of biasing his colleagues against the family, or acting on gossip and hearsay. This is a difficult dilemma as one can see problems in any form of record keeping. There is some controversy over whether or not parents should be allowed to see their child's record card. It is arguable whether children's best interests would be served by allowing this on every occasion. In some countries there is a legal requirement that parents be permitted to see such records.

Home and school

During the 1960s the importance of parents was recognized more and more and the 1970s saw a considerable increase in schools establishing parent-teacher associations or involving parents in more active participation. During the 1980s parents have acquired more legal rights to choose their children's school or receive information about their progress. Successive studies of children's achievement in school, both in Britain and elsewhere, show convincingly that parent's attitudes to education are crucial. Irrespective of social class, if parents strongly support their children they do much better at school than if they show no interest.

One major stumbling block, however, is that well-meaning parents often do not know how best to help their children. We once carried out a research project at Exeter University which involved us in interviewing hundreds of parents about their children's schooling. We discovered great goodwill but massive ignorance about what was happening.

Many parents told us that they deliberately did nothing to prepare their children for school as they had been warned that they might ruin their education. We interviewed teachers to discover what it was that parents did to wreck their children's future. We got only one answer: they taught capital letters and the schools taught the small letters first!

In the light of the interviews several schools decided to write positive letters to parents telling them how they could help prepare children for school, giving tips like 'If your child is interested in learning letters teach him the small ones first', or 'Do not push your child to learn things if he does not wish, but many children enjoy helping with shopping, listening to stories, or playing games like picture Lotto, and these are all useful and pleasant ways of preparing for school'.

Other schools put on evenings for parents to discover more about their children's schooling, not in the form of long-winded talks about new curricula, but often based on activity. For example one school showed parents a videotape of a creative writing lesson to demonstrate how children's writing was nurtured. Another put parents into a room set out with junior school science experiments and invited them to pick up a card and do the little experiment on it. Parents spent the evening playing with magnets and iron filings, pouring liquids, discovering about sound and light, and were almost too absorbed to discuss their experiences.

At the end of a year of such experiments at involving parents in their children's education the reaction from teachers and parents was overwhelmingly favourable, and this a common finding. Many schools which begin apprehensively, wondering if parents will come, are delighted at the response they get.

There are some problems, however. First of all letters of invitation need to be delivered and read. Some children never give their parents the details. In multiracial schools it often helps if community leaders can translate important letters into the appropriate languages, or they may be delivered but not understood.

Second, the timing must be right. Some parents work shifts and cannot manage a 7.30 meeting, others have small children and need a creche or playgroup run by volunteers if they are to come in for an evening or afternoon meeting.

Third, the occasion must be worthwhile. The secret of the success of any schools in the Exeter research was that they really involved parents. Even at upper secondary level where the subject matter is difficult some teachers have used the assembly hall, half for the pupils to do their lesson, half for the parents to watch and eventually wander round. The annual meeting for parents, which schools have been required to hold since the 1986 Education Reform Act, has often been badly attended. One way of ensuring a better audience is to combine the formal part of the business with another event such as a concert, display of work or a chance to talk individually to teachers in their classrooms.

Even schools in difficult areas can win the support of parents. One school in a town with massive social problems ran a book club. Children brought small sums of money week by week, and at monthly intervals a good children's bookseller put on a display and they cashed in their savings after school, often with their parents in attendance. This allowed high grade reading material to reach children whose homes often contained not a single book. The reading ages of the children climbed spectacularly.

Another school used parent volunteers to collect dinner money, escort children on field trips, help with games coaching and aid teachers building up a collection of magazine articles and newspaper cuttings. With or without a parent-teacher association there is no limit to the ingenuity of teachers who really want to involve parents. The horror stories one occasionally reads of major rows between schools and parents are often, though not always, because parents have not been sufficiently informed of what the school is trying to do.

Some schools and local authorities have gone to much greater lengths than ever before to involve parents by putting on classes for them, so that they can better help their children at home. Various schemes have been launched, especially in the field of reading, but sometimes in mathematics as well. Parents are shown various methods of hearing their children read and are given appropriate books which they can read at home together. One example of such a scheme is PACT (Parents And Children and Teachers), which developed from a project first set up in some inner London primary schools in 1979 (see the bibliography for two books about PACT written by Alex Griffiths and Dorothy Hamilton).

Sometimes family workshops are arranged where several members of the family may come together to do craftwork, make music or pursue some other worthwhile activity. Despite all the work of the last few years there is still a great deal to be done before parents are fully in the picture, and many schools have already shown the way with good school reports, interesting evenings, easy informal communication and teachers who take the trouble to get to know the district and community where their children live.

Multicultural education

In many city classrooms in Britain one finds a mixture of children from all sorts of ethnic groups, from Britain, Europe, West Indies, Asia and Africa. The concept of multicultural education is that teachers will take into account their great variety of backgrounds.

If one looks at what is offered in the curriculum it sometimes has an exclusively British look about it. History, for example, may be about Sir Francis Drake, Nelson and Disraeli; religious education may deal only with Christianity; English may concern itself with Dickens, Wordsworth and Ted Hughes.

Those who advocate multicultural education are not arguing that 'if people want to live in this country they just have to fit in', nor, on the other hand, are they suggesting that the curriculum should be dominated by studies of Islam, the history of black Africa, soul music or the politics of South-East Asia, but rather that there should be some respect for the traditions of various ethnic groups, and that the commitment to mutual tolerance in our society is a worthy ideal.

There are many ways of working towards this objective. Schools often begin by involving parents of all communities in the life of the school, as described earlier in this chapter, and by recognizing important cultural differences: that certain foods may not be eaten, that girls are not allowed out unescorted at night in some cultures, that families may wish to observe their own religious festivals.

Another possibility is to feature the customs of various groups

138

in some public way, so that children may perform folk dances, sing songs, act plays, read poetry or show and talk about religious ceremonies in their own region. Some teachers will offer options within their course which may be of special interest to certain pupils.

In lessons like Home Economics teachers need to be aware that some children will be vegetarians or like food cooked with certain spices. Sausage rolls may, therefore, not be something which all families will eat. In science lessons food testing can involve tropical fruits like mangoes as well as the usual foods.

Some teachers will go even further and attempt to tackle directly issues such as racial prejudice with classes. This needs skilful handling, but if well done can contribute a great deal to harmonious race relations in a community.

The need for children to understand the lives and beliefs of others is not confined to large industrial cities with multiethnic communities. In schools in areas sometimes referred to as the 'white Highlands' children need to develop a broad perspective and an understanding of life in other parts of Britain and other countries where political, religious and social beliefs may be different from our own. There is no need to undertake this broader study at the expense of understanding our own culture. It would be as wrong to ignore the fact that Christianity has long been the predominant religion in Britain as it would be to pretend there is no other faith in the world; as foolish to ignore British history, geography and culture as to neglect the world perspective.

Integrating children with special educational needs

The education of mentally and physically handicapped children is an important matter which has received a great deal of publicity in recent times. Some of the debate has centred around the question of whether such children should be taught in special schools or with the rest of their group in ordinary primary and secondary schools. For some years now the word 'handicapped' has been replaced by the term 'special educational needs' (SEN).

One problem which has bedevilled special education for years is the low aspiration which adults have had for SEN children. For fear of expecting too much they have sometimes expected too little. Those who believe in integration often argue that children's horizons would be raised in normal schools, whereas critics of integration feel that the opposite might occur; they might become overawed by their high-achieving fellows and opt out altogether. The Warnock Report in 1978 and the 1981 Education Act endorsed the notion that children with special educational needs should be integrated into ordinary schools where this made good sense. There are different kinds of integration, from permanent ordinary classes but with proper support facilities, to classes containing only special education pupils but with the possibility of social contacts with the other children in the school. Alongside integration, a certain number of special schools still feature prominently in the provision for children with special educational needs.

Some countries have already integrated most, if not all, SEN children into ordinary schools. It has been done some time, for example, in Sweden, and there has been some considerable movement towards integration in many regions of the United States, so that one might find large numbers of such pupils in ordinary schools, many with cerebral palsy or more severe problems.

When integration takes place there are several implications for schools. Premises may need altering to take wheelchairs or be safer for the blind, teachers need to learn about mental and physical handicap, specialist teachers need to be available who have been properly trained in the field, and close liaison with medical and social services is essential.

Furthermore the many specialist organizations for blind, deaf and other specific handicaps need to be mobilized. Most people are often astonished, for example, to discover how many books have been put on cassette or produced in Braille editions, and how many aids are available from the various providers, until they encounter a blind or deaf person for the first time. Although the process of integration has been daunting and there is not universal agreement about its desirability, those many schools and colleges which have completed the process have frequently, albeit after an initially difficult period, become very committed to their policy. In schools where significant numbers of SEN children are to be found it is worth considering having on the governing body someone from the area health authority staff to facilitate communication between the health and education services.

Disruptive pupils

'I don't know what to do with him, but if anyone else tells me he's from a difficult home background I shall scream', said one teacher after dealing with a very anti-social fourteen-year-old boy. This is the dilemma a classroom teacher faces, on the one hand feeling sorry for someone who in his family life is clearly up against it, on the other hand angry at his bullying, vile language or interruption of others going peacefully about their business.

There are several kinds of disruptive pupil and many different ways of dealing with severe disruption. We are referring here not to the mild bit of cheek or inattention one finds everywhere at some time, but to the kind of pupil whose name is on every teacher's lips, and who has the ability, in full flow, to bring lessons to a complete standstill.

Disruptive behaviour is not usually caused by a single factor. For example, one might say that a pupil who does not understand what is happening in lessons will become anti-social, but there will be several others in a similar position who merely stare into space uncomprehendingly. It is usually some combination, therefore, of elements such as boredom, dislike of school in general or a teacher or other pupils in particular, problems at home, and an aggressive or attention-seeking personality, which produces disruption.

Sadly, violent behaviour does appear to run in families, and parents who beat their children have often been subjected in their childhood to brutality by their own parents. A child used to the rule of the fist can be extraordinarily difficult to handle, as school sanctions are far less punitive than what he is used to, and he may simply not know yet how to respond to kindness and interest, having not encountered them before.

One remedy frequently tried is to ignore bad behaviour, but respond favourably and publicly to good behaviour, however unspectacular it may be. In some schools both in Britain and the United States there has been some success with reward systems whereby badly behaved pupils are given tokens for listening to others, waiting their turn, sitting still, getting on with their work and so on, eventually being allowed to cash in their tokens for prizes such as privileges or sweets. Perhaps obesity and dental decay are a fair swap for disruptive behaviour.

Amongst other ideas found in schools is a 'time out' or 'sin bin' system. As some disruptive pupils are hyperactive and quick to lose their self-control, a cooling off period can sometimes help. The pupil leaves the classroom to go to a special unit with a teacher particularly skilful at dealing with difficult pupils. After a short or longer interlude he returns to his class. This method can work well but it needs extraordinarily sensitive handling, otherwise weak teachers opt out of their responsibilities, and the system becomes a game.

In some schools teachers become very punitive, using the whole range of agreed school sanctions: withdrawal of privileges, detention or extra work. Although this too can occasionally be effective it can also result in an even more sullen and anti-social pupil, and many teachers prefer trying to win the child's confidence and respect, however wearing this may be.

Indeed some of the more notable successes have been achieved by teachers who have struggled to get through to very disturbed pupils, sometimes with the assistance of the child guidance service. There has been a significant change in the way many schools psychologists prefer to work. Whereas formerly it was accepted that problem children would be taken out of school and sent to a clinic where the psychologist would work her wizardry, a number of specialists in child guidance, though by no means all, prefer now, wherever possible, to work with the teachers in the school and tackle the problems where they occur. When this works well teachers and psychologists find they have a much higher regard for each other, and a better understanding of what needs to be done both to help the disruptive pupil and protect his fellows.

If all else fails there are still some possible lines of attack. A child may be transferred to another school, which, though it often merely passes on the problem, can occasionally give a genuinely fresh start. If a child is judged to be seriously maladjusted he may be sent to a specialist school for maladjusted children or to a school which has a special unit if one is available in the district.

Should the pupil be in trouble with the police the child's future may in any case be in the hands of the courts if he is to be put into care or sent away into detention. If there is a problem in the child's whole family, there is a new and now well-established tradition in some areas of whole family treatment using psychiatric social workers if necessary.

No-one should underestimate, however, the wear and tear on the whole community, teachers and pupils alike, caused by the presence of one or two really disruptive pupils. There are no easy solutions, and the problems of disaffection, violence and anti-social behaviour, especially amongst adolescents of fourteen or fifteen, remain amongst our most pressing social problems. Some teachers believe that discipline has become harder to establish and maintain in recent years, though this is hard to prove.

Formal or informal?

Amongst issues which regularly arouse discussion in the press is the question of teaching methods. Is traditional teaching better than progressive teaching? Are formal methods better than informal methods? The debate was fuelled in 1976 by the appearance of Neville Bennett's Lancaster study in which he found that children taught formally in the primary school did better on tests of basic skills than those taught informally (*Teaching Styles and Pupil Progress*, Open Books, 1976).

Definitions of 'traditional' and 'progressive' or 'formal' and 'informal' are not commonly agreed, but there are some features one can describe. At its crudest a formal style implies rows of desks facing the front, the teacher addressing the whole class, all the children engaged on the same task, no freedom of movement without the teacher's permission, stress on competition and academic achievement, and regular testing.

An equally rough and ready caricature of informal teaching suggests tables placed around the room in no particular order, children working individually or in small groups, the teacher walking around monitoring what they are doing, freedom for children to go to the resources area, to paint, do maths, pursue their project, or to read as they decide, stress on co-operation and social development, and individual records of each child's progress.

One reason why the discussion sometimes causes wrath is that we all like to believe we were fairly well educated, or at least that what happened to us did us no harm, and that anything different might be an experiment on children, a raw deal for society, or even a needless risk.

As ever, the argument often centres around stereotypes which barely exist. Most teachers use a mixture of styles, addressing the

143

whole class when appropriate, sometimes working in groups, allowing freedom of movement in certain phases of the lesson but not others, and determining what children do on some occasions whilst allowing choices on others. Fears that the education system is saturated with way-out informal teachers whose classes never do any decent work are exaggerated.

Estimates of the spread of informal teaching vary between one in six and the one in twenty reported in the DES primary school survey in 1978. Furthermore some informally taught classes work very hard indeed, and in the Neville Bennett study it was an informal teacher whose class showed the highest gains in achievement out of the whole sample.

Teachers can often succeed using any style of teaching to which they are strongly committed. What is critical is not so much the style, but the skill with which it is applied. Informal teaching is very difficult to do well and demands a great deal of the teacher, who needs good class management, great mobility, proper record keeping and considerable inventiveness.

We once did a case study of the informal teacher whose children obtained highest gains in the Bennett study. She had excellent relationships with her class, and ensured that everyone worked hard by getting around to every pupil and sometimes publicly taking stock. She would, for example, review progress by saying suddenly, 'Now you two are doing your maths, and John and Peter you're still working on assembly, Mary I think it's probably about time you were leaving that'. It was a light touch but everyone knew that she had a complete grasp of each child's progress. The work-rate of her pupils was the highest we ever recorded in either a formal or an informal classroom.

It is true, unfortunately, that the lessons of teachers who attempt informal teaching and are not able to handle it with skill can be very unproductive. Children slow-time the teacher by spinning out a half-hour task into a half or whole day, and learn very little else, other than to dislike the school. Equally, however, an unskilled formal teacher can bore children to distraction by talking most of the time and allowing little or no individual work.

At the heart of skilful informal teaching often lies sensitive handling of project work. A project is undertaken either by the whole class or on an individual or small group basis. Thus a primary school class may spend a few weeks doing a project on

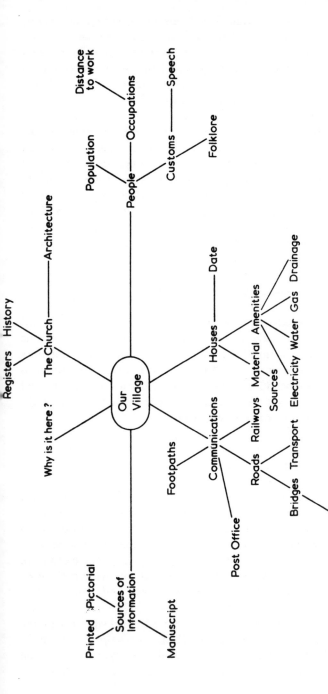

Figure 13 A project diagram showing how the topic Our Village might be studied (from *Changing the Primary School*, John Blackie, Macmillan, 1974).

'our village', but individuals may opt for something of personal interest like 'horses', 'railways' or 'farming' (see Figure 13).

By devoting a considerable amount of time to projects which have captured their imagination children will read and write a great deal, and will have to learn how to find and use information, as well as how to organize their time. A teacher's scheme for a class project on 'our village' shows how wide-ranging the topic can be when properly planned and thought out.

The formal versus informal debate will continue, but no-one has yet proved conclusively that a way of operating by itself is critical. The Bennett study was based on only twelve formal and thirteen informal teachers, and the superiority of the formally taught group is in doubt not only because of the smallness of the sample, but also because the samples were not properly matched at the outset, the formally taught classes having a higher initial achievement than the informally taught ones.

Nevertheless the Bennett study was a well conducted piece of research, and questions about teaching methods must always be asked by both professionals and the lay public. Such questioning is entirely healthy provided that sensibly worked out new teaching methods, thought to be more effective, or more suitable to changed conditions or improvements in our knowledge, are permitted. Schools where nothing changes are as undesirable as those where nothing is ever the same, and new methods can only prove themselves if given a decent chance to run and if subjected to regular and deliberate evaluation.

Grouping for teaching and learning

'Setting', 'streaming', 'banding', 'mixed ability teaching' are all terms used to describe how children are grouped in schools. Most primary schools use classes of mixed ability, and in recent years this pattern has spread to a number of secondary schools. It is perhaps most helpful to give a short description of the meaning of each of these terms, in so far as there is any agreement about them, and to mention some advantages and disadvantages commonly attributed to each.

Streaming was for many schools the traditional way of grouping pupils. Some indication of *general* ability was sought; it might be the result of an intelligence test or, more likely it would be the child's performance in end of year exams. Thus the brightest children were put into the A stream, the next brightest into the B stream, and so on, right down to the D or E stream, or even the fourteenth or fifteenth stream in a few very large secondary schools. The advantages seemed to be that the teacher, having a thin band of ability range in his class, could keep children occupied at the appropriate level, stretching the brightest and moving slowly with lower streams. Critics argued that the system was insensitive, as some pupils are good at maths, poor at French or vice-versa, and led to the 'self-fulfilling prophecy' whereby children in the D stream, feeling they are the 'sink' or the 'thickies' become anti-social and unambitious. A further problem was the low transfer rate between streams, which meant people placed in a low or high stream were probably destined to stay there.

Setting was partly designed to combat criticism of the insensitivity of streaming by general ability and is a form of streaming by *specific* ability. A child may be in set 3 for English, set 1 for maths, set 2 for French, set 5 for science, and so on. Objectors argue that some children are put in high sets for everything and others in low sets for all their lessons, so the 'sink' mentality and the self-fulfilling prophecy still apply, the bright get better and the dull are given lower horizons and still become anti-school.

Mixed ability was an attempt to give everyone a fair chance by having classes containing the whole ability range found in the school. Thus on intake children will be put randomly into classes all containing a mixture of backgrounds and abilities. It was hoped that this would remove the difficult D stream problem, and avoid the premature labelling of children as bright or dull at an age when poor self-esteem might crucially affect learning. Critics of mixed ability grouping argue that the assignment is too difficult for most teachers, that bright children become bored, and the less able are left behind as the teacher struggles to cater for the average pupil. They also point to the massive amount of preparatory and recording work necessary if the teacher is to do mixed ability teaching sensitively, ensuring each child is engaged in something appropriate to his ability and interests. Most primary school classes are now of mixed ability and there is continuing argument about how far it should spread into secondary schools.

Banding is for many schools a compromise between streaming and mixed ability teaching. Sympathizing with some of the aspirations of mixed ability enthusiasts, but not wishing to span the whole ability range, they operate usually via two or three broad bands of ability. For example a school with an entry of eight classes of children each year may have three bands, band 1 containing three classes of brighter children, band 2 with three classes of average ability, and band 3 having two classes of slower learners. Within each band the classes are of equal ability and take parallel courses. The argument advanced against banding is that it still labels children as A, B or C.

Other possibilities. People can be grouped for learning in any way one chooses. For many years children were grouped by *sex* with boys and girls educated separately. We take it for granted that children of the *same age* should be educated together irrespective of their ability yet in some primary schools 'vertical' or 'family' grouping is practised, whereby 5- to 7-year-olds are put together, and there has been a remarkable breed of practitioner in one- and two-teacher rural schools who has coped with 5 to 11 or even 5- to 15-year-olds in the same class. In smaller sixth forms 16- to 19-year-olds may be in the same group, and adult education caters for evening classes containing adolescents, the middle-aged and retired people, from 13 or 14 up to 70 or 80.

Teachers of mathematics and French often opted out of the mixed ability pattern (though a few did not with conspicuous success) on the grounds that these are linear-subjects. In order to learn B you must have learned A first, it was said; and certainly it is the case that in most secondary schools which do have mixed ability classes for the first two or three years the mathematicians and linguists are likely to prefer setting from the beginning or after the first year.

Successful teachers of mixed ability classes use a judicious mixture of whole class teaching, individual and small group work, and spend many hours creating workbooks, workcards, and resource material. Almost invariably they keep detailed records of children's work.

There can be no hard and fast rule about grouping children for learning, what suits one school is simply not appropriate for another. A key factor, however, is the commitment of those who have to work the system.

Specialization

By comparison with many other countries the British educational system is very condensed, and this has partly been due to early specialization which has narrowed choices for pupils at 13 or 14 by asking them to choose between, say more science, another language and practical subjects. Thus the third year secondary pupil would be making a critical decision which might already be determining whether he will eventually join the Arts or Science sixth form.

At the 16-plus stage he will probably specialize in two, three or four subjects (whereas his counterpart in many European countries or in the USA would still be studying in several fields), and at 18 he may go on to complete a three-year degree programme. Meanwhile a similar student elsewhere might at 19 embark on a four-year degree course, or, in Germany for example, on an open-ended university career which might last for at least six or seven years. This early specialization in Britain produces graduates at 21 as compared with 23-, 24- or 25-year-old graduates abroad.

Critics of early specialization have tried to secure a broader curriculum through revision of the examination system. Various sixth form examination patterns have been proposed over the years, some necessitating an Arts/Science mix, others requiring the sixth former to take exams at two levels, say some 'A' levels and further 'O' levels, or, as in the Schools Council proposals made in the late 1970s, three subjects at Normal (N) and two at Further (F) level. Some educationists favour the pattern of the International Baccalaureate, which not only requires pupils to study a wider range of subjects, but has an added recommendation of being widely accepted abroad in an age when international recognition of qualifications obtained in various countries is becoming increasingly important.

In 1988 the Higginson Committee recommended that sixth formers should take five equally weighted subjects, but the government said it preferred a mixture of traditional 'A' levels and the Advanced Supplementary (A/S) level examination.

The National Curriculum, by requiring all pupils to take a science or language up to the age of 16, has reduced some aspects of early specialization. Nevertheless, unexciting science teaching and outstanding English teaching in a school may produce a dearth of science and a glut of English specialists. Similarly strong sex stereotyping, whereby it is subtly suggested that girls ought not to do science, for example, can bring about the situation which has occurred in Britain, producing three or four times as many boys taking 'A' level Physics as girls. Yet in other countries girls may take science on the same scale as boys and go on in sizeable numbers to become engineers, technicians or nuclear physicists. The Equal Opportunities Act, which made it illegal for someone to be denied the opportunity to take a subject on offer in the school on the grounds of sex alone, as well as some changes in attitude generally, have led to more girls specializing in science and technology in recent times.

Tests and examinations

The concern for accountability in education often tends to focus on examinations and testing. Tests, it is argued, will show whether or not schools are delivering the goods, and there is some support for this idea. Dissenters, on the other hand, point to the evils of the 'payment by results' system in use before the turn of the century, when schools for poorer children in city centres were starved of resources and this served to compound rather than alleviate children's misfortune. One of the concerns, mentioned above, about the proposals in the 1988 Education Act for tests at 7, 11, 14 and 16 was that badly handled, it might lead to a two- or three-tier system with parents flocking to the upmarket, high-scoring schools.

In the 1960s and 1970s there was a massive shift in the public examining pattern. The 11+ examination, designed to help local authorities assign pupils to secondary schools, declined sharply as comprehensive reorganization spread, but the 16+ increased considerably over the same period. Whereas formerly about 20 to 25 per cent of the age group would take a public examination like the GCE, once CSE had been set up, ostensibly for children in the middle band of ability, the position changed rapidly. By the late 1980s about 90 per cent of pupils were leaving school having taken 'O' level or CSE examinations. The fusion of GCE and CSE, the General Certificate of Secondary Education (GCSE), produced its first cohort in 1988. It was a radically different examination which stressed enquiry and investigation in fields like mathematics or science, and skill at communication in modern languages. Marks obtained for coursework could contribute to the final grade, and this was typically a fifth or a quarter but could even be, in the case of an English syllabus, for example,

100 per cent. The pressure on pupils and teachers is quite considerable in such an examination.

The examination for 17-year-olds, the Certificate in Prevocational Education (CPVE), is another radical kind of assessment based on profiles rather than on three-hour examinations. The Advanced Supplementary (A/S) level, equivalent to half an 'A' level, is another product of the 1980s proliferation of public examinations.

Clearly, too strong an emphasis on testing would produce a very narrow curriculum with teachers under pressure to coach for the test. On the other hand a sensible programme of testing can provide useful measures of the extent to which knowledge and skills are being acquired, attitudes are changing, or objectives are being realized.

There have been several new technical developments in testing in the last few years. Whereas in the past many examinations consisted exclusively of essay questions, amongst techniques currently used are:

Oral tests	Interviews with pupils, tape-recording of conversations in a foreign language etc.
Multiple choice tests	The pupil has to circle the correct answer from a set of several possibilities, only one of which is correct, the others acting as distractors, e.g.

Britain declared war on Germany in 1939 because:

A The Archduke of Austria was assassinated by a German.
B Germany and Austria signed a treaty
C U-boats had been sinking British passenger ships.
D Hitler occupied Poland and refused to withdraw
E German planes bombed London.

Graded tests	Like the driving test these are pass/fail tests, sometimes called criterion-referenced tests. Instead of gaining a mark out of 100 the pupil simply passes or fails and may take the examination again until successful. Certain examinations have always been organized like this and the idea is spreading. In French, for example, level 1 might be an indication of the pupil's understanding of simple French, level 2 the pupil's ability to sustain

151

simple conversation on everyday topics, level 3 being able to translate for a friend, and so on.

In 1988 the Task Group on Assessment and Testing (TEGAT) produced a report proposing that the national tests at 7, 11, 14 and 16 required by the 1988 Education Act should use a ten point scale. Seven year old pupils would probably score at Levels 1, 2 and 3; children aged eleven at roughly Levels 3, 4, or 5, perhaps even 6; children aged fourteen might achieve at Levels 4, 5, 6 and 7; and at age sixteen, the highest grades would coincide with the GCSE grades. Pilot tests were scheduled to begin in 1991 and the full programme of testing in 1992.

Changing pupil numbers

Until the late 1970s most people thought that falling rolls were what you got when the baker's delivery boy dropped his basket. They were much more devastating than that.

From 1954 to 1964 the birth figures climbed steadily, reaching around 900,000 in 1964. Each year after that they dropped steadily and then sharply, falling below 600,000 in the late 1970s and producing the lowest birth cohorts since the 1930s when some people thought that the British people would be extinct by the year 2000. From 1977 they rose again.

The consequences are clear to see. When the birth figures drop by over one third in quite a short time the effects are bound to ripple right through the education system. First of all primary school rolls fell in the 1970s as the leaner years began to enter full-time schooling. Secondary school rolls reached peak size in 1978 or1979 but numbers must now fall until the mid-1990s. Higher education will be affected in the 1990s. Teacher training was also decimated as fewer teachers were required, and many colleges of education were forced to close or merge with universities or polytechnics.

In primary schools the effects were considerable but manageable, as the one teacher one class system allowed natural wastage when someone left or retired. In secondary schools, where most teachers are subject specialists, the effects are worse. Promotion is harder to come by, the school may no longer be able to offer all it could when it was larger, and early retirement and redundancies have to be faced.

Falling rolls will have different effects on different schools. A secondary school of 900 pupils, in an inner-city area where the population is moving away or being rehoused, may fall to 300 pupils or be closed down. In a more typical area it will drop to 600 pupils. On the other hand, if sited in a new town, near an expanding housing estate or a popular suburb, it may stay at 900 or increase to over 1000.

Rising enrolments began to affect primary schools from 1985. Rising rolls usually bring a need for temporary classrooms, more teachers and resources, and more new schools.

Governors will, however, hear most about rising numbers in the primary field and falling rolls in the secondary sector, and this may be their most pressing organizational problem. Those who are not too old might consider breeding for Britain, on the grounds that each new child will provide employment for a twentieth of a teacher or so, and help look after the rest of us in our old age when all the low birthrate years have to work like two people to pay for our vitamin pills and false teeth.

A school on the run

All the issues depicted above pale into insignificance when a school becomes the victim of adverse publicity and finds itself on the run. The effect on staff, pupils, parents and the whole community can be considerable and the mass media play an important role.

The relationship between the educational system and the media is a curious one. For some reason bad news about schools is good news for newspapers, so that teachers are often dismayed when the local press, having ignored all their exam results, the pupils who painted old people's bungalows, or collected a million lollipop sticks for Oxfam, devote half a page to the school's one glue sniffer.

William Taylor, writing about the press's negative reaction in the first years of the secondary modern school, cited many extracts from newspaper cuttings in the early days which gleefully emphasized vandalism, low standards or pieces of scandal. Comprehensive schools have suffered in the same way, as have informal teaching methods and certain new curricula.

One of the present writers was concerned with an independent enquiry into a school set up in response to huge press coverage of

153

criticisms by a small group of parents. Newspapers had devoted pages to the accusations, TV and radio had covered the setting up of the enquiry and national politicians who had never been within 100 miles of the school were calling for dismissals and resignations. When the report of the independent group was published stating that there was no substance to the accusations and that the overwhelming majority of parents supported the school, no national paper showed any interest and TV and radio were silent. Only the local newspapers carried brief reports.

Consequently it is vital for all schools to have good relations and effective communication between staff, parents, local and regional media and governors. It is quite common for governors, head, teachers or parents to be interviewed when some problem has occurred, and if public strife is fuelled it is hard for the school to recover and for scars to be healed.

When angry people write to MPs or the Secretary of State, demand enquiries, say in the press or on TV that they are 'appalled' or 'disgusted', something has gone seriously awry. It could happen to any school one day no matter how carefully it goes about its business, and in tightly-knit communities the people concerned may never recover. It is therefore crucial for governors to take advice from their fellows, from teachers and the head and from people knowledgeable about schools in general or about the events concerned in particular before expressing opinions publicly which may be based on inaccurate or erroneous information. The skilful use of local newspapers, radio and television is most important. If there has been plenty of good news a school can weather a single piece of bad luck.

7

Difficult situations

In this section we have included some of the things that can happen to you as a governor, and suggest some ways in which you might react. The answers are not by any means clear cut, and it is up to you to use your judgement.

It would be a useful exercise for you first to read the 'problem' and try to use your commonsense on it. Then read our comments and see how they compare with your own judgement. Sometimes our comments are very brief, but where the problem is complex our commentary is accordingly fuller.

These are all, incidentally, based on real-life events which have come before governing bodies for discussion or decision.

Accidents to pupils

Problem There has been an injury to a pupil during the school day. The head reports to the governors' meeting that the child was taken promptly to hospital, but the parents have decided to sue for negligence.

Comment Sadly, every year children of school age are injured in accidents, most only very slightly. When this happens in school the staff fill out accident report forms which may well be mentioned at your meetings. Very occasionally you may be told that parents have actually consulted solicitors about legal action: for that reason it is worth your while to know something about the law relating to accidents in school. There is no need to feel very worried about this, as you are unlikely to be involved directly, and the matter will be handled by legal experts of the LEA. However, in view of the possible high costs to parents were a child paralysed after a rugby accident, for example, it is important for governors to make sure there is proper insurance cover for games, school trips or any potentially hazardous activity. This is usually paid for by parents as part of the costs of a school journey.

Accidents happen in the street and at home as well as in school and the overwhelming majority are nobody's fault. However, if parents believe that the accident to their child could reasonably have been foreseen or prevented by the school, they are entitled to sue for damages in the courts.

Parents of injured pupils are understandably upset and often angry. Sometimes the injuries can be very severe indeed. However, it is up to them to prove their case, and in law the extent of the injury has nothing to do with whether the teacher or the school is responsible. Obviously, if liability is proved, the compensation awarded will be much greater for severe injury.

Teachers are expected to take as much care of the pupils as reasonable parents would, and this is the test that the courts apply. However, they recognize that the circumstances in the hurlyburly of school are different from life at 27 Lilac Avenue. At home there are usually only one or two children to be looked after by one or two adults, at school children move in groups of twenty and thirty or more, usually under the supervision of only one teacher. Because of the larger numbers, the likelihood of a genuine accident occurring is greater. Larking about and horse-play are an accepted part of a child's growing up. It is up to the courts to say in each case whether they think that the larking about was excessive and should have been stopped. If, for example, in icy weather children make a slide across the playground and one of them falls and is injured, the law would probably take the view that such normally harmless activities have been enjoyed by youngsters since time began: indeed the same pupils who make one slide at lunchtime in the playground probably make another at home the same evening, and parents might even join in, so an accident of that sort does not justify compensation merely because it happened during school hours.

Of course the parents may well argue that they have always kept their child away from such slides, have been known to punish him (in his own interests) when he has dashed along one. To them, the school has not behaved in the way that they as reasonable parents would.

The law's reply is that the school's job would be quite impossible if each and every child had to be treated in exactly the manner required by its parents. For one thing, would that apply equally to very bad parents, and who would decide whether they *were* good or bad? Furthermore, the teacher is an additional parent to a whole group of children, and has to consider what is good for his 'family' as a whole, and not only for one of its members. It is up to the courts of law then to say what a reasonable action would be in each case that comes along. A father cannot dictate to a teacher how his child should be treated, any more than he can dictate to his wife, or godparents.

It would in theory be possible to prevent all accidents in schools. One way would be to remove anything that could cause injury. Top of the list would be opening doors, followed by glass windows. After that we would remove all chairs to prevent pupils falling over backwards, and all desks to prevent fingers being trapped. Scissors, compasses, fountain pens, oil-cans, chisels, swimming baths and football pitches, language laboratories and most certainly science labs would all have to go. And we could pass a law making it necessary to search all pupils twice daily for concealed weapons like nail files, penknives and the vicious conker. Accidents would stop, but so would schools and education.

Despite all this, parents are sometimes advised that their school has not lived up to the standards of care required, and that the pupil has a chance of being awarded compensation in court. It is not malice or a wish to get back at someone that makes parents go through the lengthy, time-consuming and above all expensive legal processes. Rather it is the sheer necessity of now having to provide, perhaps, a life-time's care for a handicapped child. What, for example, of the brilliant pianist whose hand may be damaged permanently one day in the chemistry laboratory because his teacher made a mistake?

Parents usually take teachers' employers to court, because the law holds the employer responsible for accidents caused by his employees. As we have seen, it is the LEA which is the employer in county schools. In the case of voluntary aided schools the situation is more complicated. Although the governors are actually the employers, the law makes the LEA responsible for maintaining the school, so that the LEA gets caught here too!

Clearly, even though the LEA may be forced to pay damages, perhaps running into many thousands of pounds, the teacher certainly does not escape scot-free. His professional reputation suffers very badly and the wear and tear on everyone's nerves waiting for a court judgement – which can take literally years to be given – is enormous (and, of course, is just the same if the teacher is finally held not to have been responsible). The LEA might also decide, in the meantime, that the teacher is too expensive to keep on their staff . . .

If the teacher's negligence were gross in the extreme, the courts could make the teacher himself pay part or all of the damages, but we know of no case where this has happened. Presumably if a teacher were, on his own, to take 100 five-year-olds on a day trip to London and leave them at King's Cross with a cheery wave and a reminder to meet him there next Tuesday, such a case would merit severe treatment of the teacher, and not the LEA.

Before leaving this subject, it is necessary again to draw attention to the Health and Safety at Work Act, 1974. Your LEA will have advised the school about its policy, and you should make sure that you know what it is and the part you play. It is no use waiting until there has been an accident to find out that you are in trouble. If your school is independent of the LEA on such matters, it is vital that you know where you stand and are covered properly. The clerk to the governors will know.

The absent teacher

Problem A teacher at your school has been absent for a week, and you are asked to consider whether the absence should be with or without salary.

It appears that he and his wife attended the funeral of his father-in-law some hundred miles away, a journey which could be accomplished in a few hours in each direction. However, after the funeral his mother-in-law was in a severely depressed state, and the teacher's wife decided that she ought to stay with her mother. The wife said that she needed her husband's support, so they both stayed for the week.

The clerk informs you that it is the policy of the authority to be sympathetic to cases of illness of 'near relatives'. There is no difficulty over two days' absence for the funeral, but you are asked to decide about the remainder of the week. The head tells you that the teacher is not hardworking, does just enough to get by in school, and is never on the premises after four o'clock.

Comment There is no simple answer to this: it would be a good idea to ask the clerk what other governors have decided in similar cases, although there is no obligation on you to follow his advice. What does seem clear, though, is that the head should not try to use your discretion in welfare cases to try to discipline mediocre teachers. There are other, direct ways of doing that. In any case, the head is in charge of 'internal management and organization'.

The late arrival

Problem A young teacher has been away from your school for a

"VERY WELL, MR. JONES, I'LL PUT YOUR REQUEST TO ATTEND A FAMILY BEREAVEMENT WITHOUT LOSS OF SALARY TO THE NEXT GOVERNORS' MEETING"

year on a course, for which permission was properly granted. At the beginning of the school year in September the teacher arrives back several days late. When questioned by the head, the teacher explains that he rang the school three times during August to find out when the term started and was unable to get through. The head confirms that on the dates the teacher rang the school there was no-one present to answer the phone. Should the teacher be paid for his days of absence?

Comment Of course not. The teacher had a whole year to establish when he should be back at work, and hardly expected to find anybody there during August. Dates of terms in any case are published at least a full year in advance.

'Shall we let him in?'

Problem Your primary school is very popular and has no room left for additional pupils. Accordingly you have decided that no child shall be admitted below the age of five. A family moves into a house very close to your school; the child is under five, but has been at another school since he was four. Should he be admitted to your school?

Comment Obviously, in letting the child in to your school there is the risk that other parents living nearby with children under five will feel aggrieved. First see if there is another school available and willing to take the child. It is just possible that the authority might be willing to help with transport costs if these are involved. If these possibilities do not work out, you ought probably to admit the child and pray that twenty more cases do not come up at your next meeting. The child's interests should always come first, and it would be harmful to interrupt a child's education at the crucial time when it is first separated formally from its home background.

The 1988 Education Act laid down that a school is full only when it has reached the number of pupils it had in 1979, a boom year for pupils. Your opinion as governor about whether you are full is of no importance unless you can persuade your LEA and the DES to set a lower figure. Even so, a parent can go to appeal, and, if he is successful, you will have to admit the child over and above any limit. The Appeal Tribunal will investigate the situation at your school very fully, however.

160

'I'm not having anyone tell me what my Elvis should wear!'

Problem In an attempt to smarten up your school you have agreed to support the head in introducing school uniform. You are generally successful in this and the idea is popular with parents. However, Mrs Hittemback insists on sending her Elvis to school every day in the most outrageous clothes and the boy, encouraged by his mother, is truculent about the matter and encourages his friends to refuse to wear their uniform. The head delivers Elvis an ultimatum: next time he arrives at school without uniform, he will be sent home again. The head warns you about this in advance and asks for your support.

Comment Be very careful about this one. The head is technically well within his rights, and technically also does not need to consult you beforehand either. The head is responsible for making and enforcing school rules, and obviously the school would collapse if different rules applied to each child. The courts would probably support the head.

However, what good would come of a confrontation with the Hittembacks? Elvis would miss school for some time, and probably get into mischief when the novelty wore off. Mrs Hittemback would tell her story to a local reporter who may well see considerable column mileage in the 'poor devoted mother ground down by heartless bureaucrats' (yourselves) story.

The social climate in many areas would be unlikely to support you in such disciplinary measures over a matter like school uniform. Even if you did the instinctive thing and supported your head you might find County Hall breathing down your neck, if for example, the local authority supported Mrs Hittemback and did not approve of school uniform anyway. In short: try to avoid confrontation.

However, since the school has a responsibility for the safety of its pupils, you would be justified in supporting a ban on articles of dress which are likely to be dangerous in the school situation if not at home. Sky-larking boys grabbing at girls' necklaces or long earrings can do a lot of foreseeable damage. Similarly, high heels are dangerous in stampedes downstairs at lunchtime, and long hair even more so in workshops. This is not a matter of uniform, but of safety.

Under the Education Act 1986, a headteacher can exclude (terms such as 'expulsion' or 'suspension' which we all remember from school have now gone) a pupil for up to five days in one term without reference to anyone. For longer periods, or if the pupil is likely to miss the opportunity to take a public examination, the matter must go before you as governors. The parents can appeal to you, and, if you agree, you can instruct the head teacher to reinstate the pupil. The parents can also appeal to the LEA who, if they agree, can order you to take Elvis back. . . .

'I don't care if he does smoke. Mind your own business!'

Problem Your school sets particular store by the good behaviour of its pupils, and has a no smoking rule. One day a teacher leaving school sees a 16-year-old on his way home being offensive to people who live nearby and smoking. The next day the boy is punished by the head, and his father complains to you that he doesn't mind his son smoking and regularly gives him cigarettes. Furthermore, according to him, the people the boy had been insulting were well-known cranks and were always treating pupils unfairly. The father says that he intends to keep his son away from school until the head apologizes and wants the governors to bring pressure to bear.

Comment Stay well away from this one too if you can. It is a fact of British law that when a parent sends his child to a school he is deemed to have accepted the rules of the school. In some ways it is hard on parents when they have a legitimate objection to some rule and it is not possible for their child to go to another school. But the correct thing to do is for them to see the head and try to get the rule changed, and certainly not encourage their son to defy the rules so blatantly. They could also ask you to help, since governors have a responsibility for discipline in the school.

Also, British teachers are considered to be more like parents than public officials. It follows then that social training is part of a teacher's job, just as it is a parent's duty. The head was thus justified in taking action.

Whether the punishment for being rude was justified or not is more difficult. It is not necessary for the head to hold a court of enquiry and go to great lengths to establish guilt or innocence, only to have reasonable grounds for thinking that a pupil had done something to deserve punishment. Presumably the report from the teacher was just that.

Finally, if the father carries out his threat to keep his son away from school, he will put himself legally in the wrong. There is a legal duty on parents to 'cause (their child) . . . to be educated, either by regular attendance at school or otherwise'. Ultimately he could be prosecuted and fined in the courts.

'Teacher's lost my tranny'

Problem During a governors' meeting, one of your colleagues brings up a delicate matter under 'Any other business'. He has received a complaint from Mr Jones that his son's transistor radio, a Christmas present, was confiscated by his form teacher. When the boy went to collect it after school, the teacher could not find it and said it must have been stolen. Mr Jones had written to the headmaster, who had replied that the radio had been confiscated because it had become a constant nuisance and it was no part of the teacher's job to be responsible for loss arising out of such incidents. The head would certainly not consider any compensation for Mr Jones.

Comment Your colleague has not gone about this important issue in the best way. He is certainly entitled to bring any matter up under 'Any other business', which means just what it says, but he has really tried to turn your meeting into a sudden trial of the head's behaviour, which is almost guaranteed to arouse hostility. He would have been more successful if he had first got in touch with the chair of governors (or referred Mr Jones directly to him) and let the chair decide whether or not to put the matter formally on your agenda. The chair would probably have preferred to ring the head himself and see what was afoot, and could probably have put your colleague's mind at rest before the meeting, at which all matters are minuted, even ones which seem important at first sight and turn out to be rubbish!

Despite that, the head seems to have slightly misunderstood the legal position. It is certainly true that a teacher is not responsible for everything a pupil takes to school: he may not even be aware that Mary's fountain pen is solid gold and came from Harrods. But this teacher did what a parent would have done in the same case and took the transistor into his charge. In this case, the law says that he should look after it as well as he would his own property. The law does not say that the teacher must automatically make good the loss: it says that it is up to the parent in this case to show that the teacher was careless with the transistor. This would normally be difficult to prove.

Where parents have gone to the courts of law against schools and LEAs in matters like this, they have rarely been successful. The best approach for Mr Jones would be to write to the local authority giving the full facts: County (or the governors under a scheme of local financial management) *might* consider some compensation without admitting that anyone was responsible for the loss, a so-called 'ex-gratia' payment. However, it is most likely that the indignant parent would get nothing. Had his son lost compulsory games kit, or a coat from the cloakroom, he might have been on better ground, but a transistor radio has no part in normal school life, and was not required in any way. Indeed, the cause of the trouble in the first place was that it was intentionally disruptive!

Vandalism

Problem In his report to your committee, the head reports a considerable increase in vandalism in and about the school and asks for any help you can give. He is concerned particularly about relations with the community, since he has received several complaints about malicious acts of damage committed by pupils on the way to and from school. He has punished one pupil for wilfully damaging a piece of scientific equipment lent to him, and would like you to try to get compensation for the loss from the parents. The school building, too, is frequently vandalized in the evenings and at the weekends.

Comment Sadly, this sort of item has figured prominently in recent years on governors' agendas, and unfortunately there is no simple answer. Some governing bodies have found that a special parents' meeting called by them at which the co-operation of parents is asked for has produced a notable improvement. Parents are sometimes unaware of the cost to them as tax- and rate-payers of damage to school property. Sometimes, too, such a meeting will bring to light information about the culprits upon which the school can act. If your school has a parent-teacher association a joint meeting might help.

As far as punishment is concerned, such acts committed on the journey to and from school are regarded in law as being in the first instance within the head's jurisdiction. Parents sometimes misunderstand this, but it is, nonetheless, the case. If your head feels that he can deal satisfactorily with culprits, then his advice should be followed.

However, the crime might be too serious to deal with in this way, and an approach to the parents might not be fruitful. In such cases the police may be involved, either because you choose to call them in or, more likely, because someone whose property has been damaged does it directly. Certainly if you decide to seek compensation for damage you will have to first secure a conviction in the Juvenile Court. At the moment the limit of the compensation that the court can award is £800 for each offence. Incidentally, any money received in this way may belong to your LEA as the owner of the damaged property, and not to your school. Here again the advice of the clerk will be very helpful to you.

Some schools organize voluntary patrols by parents and sometimes staff around school premises at times when they seem particularly prone to vandalism. This is not the place to comment on how successful these might be. However, it is important that the police be consulted and informed before any such operation is mounted. It is also important to clarify with your clerk what the position will be with regard to insurance. While there will probably be little difficulty in ensuring cover for accidents to authorized patrollers, say, for example, by tripping over a crate carelessly left in the playground, it is unlikely that you will be covered for the results of an attack if a surprised vandal turns nasty. In such a case you would probably have to turn to the Criminal Injuries Compensation Board.

It is worth knowing that the Local Government (Miscellaneous Provisions) Act of 1982 makes it an offence to 'create a nuisance or disturbance' on educational premises. The maximum fine is £50. The disturbance can be out of school hours and need not involve anyone from the school. You might find it worthwhile to remind the local police of this. Sometimes even they are not right up to date with the law!

Dealing with angry parents

Problem Mrs Smith and her neighbour call to see you one evening. It appears that young Peter Smith has been punished by his History teacher for larking about in class.

Mrs Smith is very angry. She tells you that the teacher is always picking on her Peter for no reason. Furthermore, everybody knows that the teacher is incapable of keeping order in class, and is always giving out punishments, except to the very big boys, who terrify him, and what's more, he does not teach proper History but all this modern rubbish. Mrs Smith goes on to say that she has been to see the head about all this, but the head would not give her much time, and later wrote to her to say that he had investigated her complaints, declared them to be unfounded, and felt the teacher had acted quite properly. He did not agree with Mrs Smith that the teacher should be sacked on the spot, and would take no further action.

Comment The best way to deal with this is to let Mrs Smith have her say (you might not be able to stop her!), but make no promises beyond perhaps saying that you will see if anything can be done. There are several reasons why you should not jump in too hastily, even if you are at first inclined to.

You do not know the full facts. When children get into trouble at school, however slight, they rarely give their parents the full facts. Sometimes, indeed, they genuinely do not hear the teacher when he tells them for the fortieth time to sit down and be quiet. The relationship between teachers, parents and children can easily become emotionally loaded for the worse as well as for the best, and in cases like Mrs Smith's it is as well to let everybody calm down before anything is done.

Mrs Smith is not being very wise when she makes such

sweeping statements about the school staff. She is perfectly entitled to tell the head privately just what she thinks of the History teacher and the school in general. But as soon as she tells anyone else, such as the neighbour, she may be called upon to defend herself in court if the head or the History teacher take action for defamation. Mrs Smith would have to show that what she said was true, and it would not be enough to say that she was angry when she spoke, or that she was merely passing on gossip. Defamation is simply the making of statements, either in writing or in speech, which might damage a person's professional standing. According to law, she need make such statements only to one person to make the matter actionable. That person might even be you and would certainly be the neighbour.

Mrs Smith ought to take her complaint, in reasonable language, to the teacher's employer. In a county school, of course, that is the LEA, and she should contact the Chief Education Officer. In an aided school, teachers are employed by the governing body, and Mrs Smith should get in touch with the chairman. If the school has a system of Local Financial Management she should go to the chairman of governors.

If it turns out, however, that what Mrs Smith says is true, the LEA or governors might consider dismissal of the teacher. Indeed, in this case the head might well come under fire also for defending the teacher as he did, for the head's first loyalty is to the pupils rather than to his colleagues, however much he wishes to stand with them.

Local authorities have the power, as do employing governors, to dismiss for any reasonable cause, and in good faith. Bad time-keeping, absence without reason, refusal to carry out reasonable instructions are some of the grounds on which a teacher, like any other employee, may be dismissed, with of course the usual right of appeal, perhaps to an industrial tribunal.

There is real difficulty, however, when one comes to dismissal for general professional incompetence. It is not that teachers have a guaranteed security of tenure: rather there is the difficulty of *proving* incompetence. A doctor, for example, may regularly administer wrong drugs or treatment, or a factory worker may produce unsatisfactory goods. In teaching, however, good personal relationships are crucial, and these are harder to evaluate. A teacher may find life in one school much more congenial than in another, and, of course, pupils' behaviour varies. A teacher who has been happy and successful in a school for some time may become less so if the school is suddenly reorganized along different lines. Quite apart from this, there is no 'right' way to teach, in the sense that there is a 'right' way to produce cars in a factory.

The most common way for LEAs to deal with this sort of problem is to delay dismissal proceedings until the evidence of incompetence is overwhelming, and helpful advice and warnings have all failed. In the meanwhile, it is possible to consider transferring the teacher to another school. In some cases this solves the problem, if the teacher settles down happily.

On the other hand the teaching profession, like any other, has its problems and incompetents, and their colleagues in the staffroom would be just as glad as you if they went. If you as a governing body are agreed that a teacher should be dismissed, you can instruct the clerk to set the wheels in motion. Be particularly careful to follow meticulously the procedure laid down. Most appeals against dismissal brought by teachers claim that the procedure was unfair or wrongly carried out, and frequently this is upheld. There is little to be gained by letting an industrial tribunal send your problem back to you with a grin on his face, a cheque for compensation in his pocket, and a massive chip on his shoulder.

Changing school policy

Problem Now that the new head of your primary school has started work, you are disturbed to find that she is not interested in the ITA (Initial Teaching Alphabet) method of teaching children to read. The school has used this method for many years and you and the parents are well satisfied. However, the head tells you in her report that the method will be discontinued from the beginning of the next school year. This bit of information leaks back to the parents and several write to you, mostly attacking the change, but several supporting the new head. When the subject comes up for discussion, the head and the teacher governors argue that it is in the best interests of the school that the system should be changed.

Comment The first question to ask, perhaps of yourself is: how could a new head be appointed without the governors knowing at the interview exactly what her views were? The basic skills of reading, writing and number work are the bread and butter of primary education, and if applicants are not questioned closely about them, they could be forgiven for thinking that parents and governors had no particular preferences. Now that she has been appointed, she is in charge of teaching methods, and could reasonably say that ITA is a matter of teaching method rather than of curriculum. Under the 1988 Education Act, governors have a more direct say in the curriculum. The Act does not mention that they should control actual teaching methods, however. Perhaps the appointments procedure needs to be revised.

However, there is no need for alarm in this case. There are several widely used methods of teaching reading and skilful teachers use them all equally effectively. Presumably your head will ensure that children are not confused by the change. Probably at first only the new arrivals will use her new scheme, and the older pupils will continue with ITA.

Nothing would be gained by insisting that the school continue with ITA if the staff, as it seems, would prefer a change. It would be a good idea to have a meeting with parents at which the new ideas could be explained, and to which parents could be invited whose children had learned to read by the methods supported by the new head. You will probably find that the fears expressed by those parents who opposed the change can be allayed.

Absenteeism

Problem Young Ira Fiddle at the age of twelve is a very talented musician and the head has given her permission to go to a music teacher every Monday afternoon. Your school has no music teacher who can help her with her violin, and the head thinks that an outside music teacher is the best solution. However, this has produced an angry complaint to you from Mrs T.E.E. Bunker. Her son is tipped to be the County Junior golf champion, but the head refused him time off to be coached (he couldn't go after school because it was getting dark too early).

Comment The head was using his discretion in the best interests of Miss Fiddle, but was, in fact, legally in the wrong. By law children must be educated '. . . by regular attendance at school or otherwise'. The courts have interpreted 'regular' as meaning 'for the whole period that the school is normally open', which means in practice fulltime from Monday to Friday. The

169

words 'or otherwise' refer to those very exceptional and rare cases where parents educate their children at home, and make no use at all of schools. Once a child is registered at a school he must attend regularly. The head should not have given permission to Miss Fiddle in the first place. In cases like hers, LEAs sometimes employ peripatetic music teachers who visit several schools in turn to give special help. Golf on the other hand would probably be regarded as outside the normal curriculum, though it might be worth a try. If you are working under a scheme of local financial management you may yourself decide to employ a teacher.

The devout teacher

Problem A teacher in your school joins a particular religious sect which requires him to be absent from school on certain feast days. He applies to you for five days of absence without pay for these feasts which are granted. Shortly afterwards he applies for more time off, but you have no more discretionary days left to award him. The application goes to County Hall, but the Chief Education Officer will not grant any more days off. The teacher nevertheless takes unauthorized leave of absence, and tells the head that he intends to take more time off.

Comment Under one of the provisions of the 1944 Education Act, a teacher may not be disqualified on religious grounds from being appointed or promoted. A teacher cannot be barred from a school solely because he or she is, say, Jewish or Catholic. The education system goes further and allows, for example, Catholics to take no part in morning assembly: this applies even to headteachers.

It would seem therefore that schools should accept that they should adapt themselves *to some extent* to the religious beliefs of teachers. However, this is a question of degree. A teacher who is continually absent cannot be said to be acting in the best interests of the children he teaches. Governors usually have power to grant a few days off for special cases, but that is usually as far as the LEA is prepared to go.

Finally it should be noted that the Act intended to stop discrimination against teachers for their religious opinions, which have little bearing on their work. Time off, however, may be seen as action not opinion. If in your view the running of the school is seriously disrupted, you would be entitled to take action for unsatisfactory attendance. Dismissal is a real possibility, as it would be in any sphere of working life.

Back to basics!

Problem A row has broken out at a governors' meeting because a local councillor has produced a petition from a group of parents claiming that 'standards have fallen' in your primary school. Apparently children are failing to do 'basic work' and are spending too much time 'messing about with unimportant things'. The head suggests that you ignore the petition.

Comment It is definitely not a good idea to ignore things like this unless they really are trivial.

Ask the head to arrange a meeting for parents (all of them, not just the ones who signed the protest) with a speaker to explain what you are trying to achieve by the curriculum in your school. Your speaker could be someone from the school, or possibly an Inspector from your LEA. Have a look at *Primary Education in England*, a report by HMIs published by HMSO in 1978, and the appropriate parts of the National Curriculum.

She isn't pulling her weight

Problem Complaints abound about one of the teachers at your school. Pupils' work isn't marked, lessons seem to be near riots, and the teacher seems uninterested in any pupils but the most able.

Comment The difficulty here is not that governors have no authority to do anything at all, for they do, after all manage schools. Moreover under schemes of local financial management (see p. 27), governors are effectively the employers of teachers, and every employer has the right reasonably to influence the way in which the job is carried out. The problem is how exactly to handle it, given that most governors are not themselves teachers and are wary about involving themselves.

In the first instance the problem is for the head – it is part of 'internal management' which heads are paid to do. If a hint or two gets no reaction from the head, you could have the matter put on the agenda for the next governors' meeting. It would perhaps be wiser to keep the item neutral in tone, for example described as 'Staff matters'. You would need to consider carefully whether the teacher governors should be asked to leave the meeting while that item is under discussion: have a look at your LEA regulations on the matter. Remember that the purpose is to ventilate the problem, and *not* to hold a disciplinary hearing: that would come under your LEA disciplinary code and is handled quite differently. You must make sure that the two are kept quite separate.

Ask the head what is happening in your school about teacher appraisal, the system by which teachers' work is regularly reviewed. Staff appraisal is relatively new to the teaching profession, although many members of other professions will themselves have experienced it at work.

You should ask what steps are being taken to give the teacher help and further training and to take the matter up with the LEA if there are difficulties of achieving it at the school. As a general principle all employees should be given full details of their alleged shortcomings and reasonable time to put things right.

If all else fails, the head or chair may have to fall back on the well-known management theory of 'Now look here, sunshine . . .' Teachers are no more exempt from this than any other employee.

Save our sixth form!

Problem As a governor of a large comprehensive with a flourishing sixth form you are disturbed to hear that the LEA proposes to 'decapitate' your school at 16 and move the sixth form to become part of a tertiary college.

Comment This sort of problem arises for LEAs when falling school rolls work their way upwards in the school. They find perhaps that some teaching groups in the sixth form are too small for comfort: it is very expensive indeed, for example, to have a sixth form group of two or three for, say, physics, when one considers that the highly expensive equipment needed could be used for a group of five times that size. It could also reasonably be argued that one can't have a worthwhile class discussion in English literature with only three pupils.

The LEA will then seek to bring all the sixth form pupils from several schools together to produce larger teaching groups and to offer a wider range of subjects. They may decide on a sixth form college or a much larger tertiary college, in which all forms of study − academic, technical, vocational, day release, full-time, part-time and so on − are brought together under one roof.

If you wish to resist this change you could do a number of things but you should first of all decide whether the reorganization would be best for your pupils, because many tertiary colleges have been very successful. If you still wish to resist, try the following:

1. Ask your MP to alert the Secretary of State to keep an eye on developments. As a general principle the DES nowadays steps in firmly on such matters only if they are likely to cost too much or there is a local outcry.

2. Your school will form part of a package with other similar schools in the reorganization. Look into the possibility of yours being left out. At the moment the DES policy is to exclude 'schools of proven worth' where it is reasonable to do so. If your sixth form has, say, 160 pupils, has a wide range of subjects on offer, has a good academic record and is well-supported, you stand a good chance of 'reprieve'. The DES will of course have to decide whether leaving you out of the package will wreck the whole thing.

3. LEAs will sometimes argue that what they have in mind is educationally desirable as well as being necessary for practical considerations, such as falling rolls. The DES on the other hand may argue that you, i.e. governors and parents, are entitled to differ; it is unreasonable that you should lose your successful and cherished school because there are logistical difficulties or different thinking elsewhere in the county. It's as if someone suggested closing Eton because there were staffing difficulties at St Cuthbert's College for Young Gentlemen in Doomshire!

4. Ensure that all the forms of reorganization possible in your area have been fully examined. Some LEAs jump to their preferred policies on political grounds because they have been given a nudge from 'upstairs' somewhere. You should ask to see all the options put to the Education Committee by your Chief Education Officer.

5. Ask to see a fairly detailed breakdown of what is to be offered in the new school. Despite grandiose assurances it might turn out to be less than you already have.

6. Does your school have any characteristics which make it desirable to retain it to ensure greater parental choice? Is it single-sex? (This is often popular with parents.) Have you built up a good recruitment among children from ethnic minorities? Are your sixth form facilities such as to create a waste of public money if they were to be discontinued?

7. You might consider 'opting out' (see p. 16) or offering to receive pupils from other schools into your sixth form. A liaison meeting with other schools affected by the changes would be a good idea. The Secretary of State is not bound, however, to allow all requests for opting out, especially if the school is thought to be too small.

8. Don't be bamboozled by a lot of talk from county hall about running costs. Your governing body will have been provided by law with a statement of the annual running costs of your school, and you will probably have discussed it with your parents at the annual governors' meeting (see p.41). Check this against the relevant parts of the estimates for the reorganization.

Feeling out of touch

Problem Several governors comment to you out of meetings that they really don't know as much as they should about their school and don't know how to find out more without taking up too much time at meetings.

Comment The Advisory Centre for Education suggests having a 'Governor of the Month' – not a prize in some competition, but a duty roster where each governor in turn agrees to be general dogs-body for the governors for a month. You would automatically be on every governors' sub-committee for that month, help out with any problems that come your way, perhaps attend a staff meeting or two, chat to parents at the school gate, go to the PTA – the list is endless.

It is sad that all too often it is assumed that these useful and highly informative jobs should be done only by the chair. Since he or she usually has many other things to do as well, spreading the effort around will probably ensure that more of these jobs are better done.

Can I see Jeremy's records?

Problem Your governing body has been under pressure for some time from Mr Postlethwaite because the head refuses to let him see his son's school records. Mr Postlethwaite is convinced that one of his son's teachers 'has it in for him', by writing unpleasant things about him in confidential school reports.

Comment If your school holds personal records about staff or pupils on computer, they must be open to inspection by the people about whom they are written. This is the major effect of the Data Protection Act.

The Act does not cover records kept in any other way, however, and the decision about confidentiality is one for you or the LEA. The arguments about whether or not to open them are fairly evenly balanced, although the tendency at the moment is towards much more openness. On the one hand there is the matter of principle that all records should be open. On the other there is the danger that records will become blander and less helpful to those who read them – including teachers who receive a pupil into their class. A sort of underground intelligence network among teachers could develop.

Records in school quite often contain highly sensitive information which is invaluable to teachers. If Fred's mind wanders in class it may be that his father regularly beats him up; Mary's odd behaviour might be connected with child abuse. If opening of the records leads to this sort of information not being available, the sufferers could be the children.

The difficulty with Mr Postlethwaite is that his mind will be put at rest only if he is allowed to see other pupils' class records as well as his son's. He wishes to make sure that his son is not being treated differently, after all. Few governors would give him access to all the records, however strongly he felt. To do so would enrage other parents who would see it as an intrusion into their privacy.

Were we right to exclude them?

Problem Several cases of pupils being excluded (formerly known as 'suspended') have been reported to you. You have become increasingly worried about the way your governing body handles parents' appeals. Your fellow governors seem to assume that the appeal is no more than an opportunity for your colleagues to show loyalty to the head, and not to find out and consider the full facts.

Comment Many governors are worried by this. The head's right is to exclude pupils pending an appeal to the governors. To reinstate a pupil after an appeal can often make you feel that you are being disloyal to a fellow governor – the head.

On the other hand, to exclude a pupil, particularly if it is to be permanent, is a very serious matter indeed. The European Convention on Human Rights, which Britain signed, says that 'no one shall be denied the right to education . . .' Although the Convention is not legally binding in the UK, its effects have already been felt when Parliament abolished corporal punishment in 1986. It would be daft to sign an agreement and then ignore it.

Governors should go into the reasons for an exclusion very carefully – if only because if there is a further appeal to the LEA, the LEA will certainly do the job properly and make you look foolish if you have overlooked something you shouldn't. At an appeal the head is not a governor, but there only to give reasons, not to judge. It is generally unwise to accept statements such as 'Sharon and Albert have been pains in the you-know-what for months' without going further into it. If that is the accusation, you need to hear at least about most of the incidents leading up to the last straw, and the wise head will have kept a detailed record. If the accusation is that Sharon has beaten up the deputy head, then that is the offence about which you need evidence.

In the vast majority of cases the head was not present at the events which caused the exclusion. He has heard about it from colleagues and of course has a lot of background information from past experience. You should therefore always get statements from the teachers actually involved; depending on the circumstances you may decide that a written statement will do. It is vital also to hear what Sharon or Albert have to say. Their parents can often cast light, although one can easily get cynical about the number of villains who are sweetness and light at home . . . (probably because they are rarely there!).

The onus is on the school to convince you. If the evidence suggests to you that the school, however well meant, has got it wrong, you have a duty to end the exclusion – as much for the sake of fair play as for Sharon or Albert. You can also change the 'sentence' if you wish. The authors have discovered that roughly ten minutes with the chair of governors can work wonders . . .

In recent years more than a few governing bodies have been exposed to a form of mild blackmail by their teaching staffs: if you reinstate Sharon or Albert, say the teachers through their elected governors, they will refuse to teach them. You should resist this firmly. Your decision must be made sensibly on the facts in the case, not on threats.

Appeals to governors are not run exactly like courts of law, but the principles of fair play observed by the courts ought to apply within reason. Remember that in law it is up to parents, governors and LEA to decide which children go to which school, not teaching staffs. If Sharon or Albert are in your school with your blessing, then it would be actionable breach of contract for individual teachers to refuse to have them in their classes. On the other hand, teachers are entitled to be upset if they are receiving no help and support from governors over difficult pupils, especially if these should be violent. The final decision on readmission lies with governors, however, not with teachers, so you must make the decision.

Reports on your school

Problem You are fully aware that the LEA has recently inspected your school, and also that HMIs have been in to look at certain aspects of the teaching. No mention of this is made on your agenda.

Comment Play merry hell with the chairman, the LEA or whomsoever you think is blocking this. You have every right in law to see *every* report about your school when it is published – and sometimes before, if it concerns a matter on which your views are necessary.

If all else fails, write and complain to the Secretary of State at the DES. That will do it.

Getting it wrong over admissions

Problem At a governors' meeting the head of your secondary school reports that she has got into difficulties over admissions of new pupils. A few months ago, when she felt that the school was already full, she started a waiting list of pupils wanting to come. Several parents on the list said that they would appeal to the governors. Before the appeals were heard two pupils had unexpectedly left the school and the head had admitted the first two from the waiting list. Now the other parents on the waiting list are furious because 'first come, first served' was not published as the way in which children are admitted to your school.

Comment In the first edition of this book we included a cartoon of a family living in a tent on a school's playing field to ensure that they were in the right catchment area to secure a place for their children.

Things are much different now (cf. p. 34). Legislation since 1980 has strengthened the hand of parents in choosing a school, and that a family lives near a school is no longer on its own an absolute guarantee of a place. Fortunately, falling rolls mean that many secondary schools have spare places, but problems tend to arise where schools are full and popular.

Every year the LEA and the governors of aided schools must publish details of 'the arrangements for the admission of pupils to schools maintained by the authority','the respective admission functions of the LEA and the governors', 'the policy followed in deciding admissions', and 'the arrangements made in respect of pupils not belonging to the area of the LEA' (Education Act 1980:8).

The quotations show that Parliament intended to make the procedure for admitting pupils much clearer than before. A few points are worth noting:

1. If you have room, you must admit. Under the Education Act of 1988 your school is full only when you have at least the number of pupils you last had in the school in 1979. This figure was fixed because school numbers at that time were at an all-time high. If yours is a new school, the number is the one you opened with.

You can admit more if you wish. At the moment the law is not quite clear, but it looks as if appeals panels may still have power to admit pupils over the limit.

2. It is not possible to keep places open for children who might arrive later. You never know who will leave.

3. Just because most children from your school normally go

on to one other (say from your infants' school to the junior school up the road), it does not mean that they all must.

4. If parents choose to leave you for any other school – including independent schools – you must co-operate fully over sending on reports, records and so on to the new school.

5. Nowadays the onus is on governors or the LEA to show why parents should *not* have their choice, and not the other way round.

6. Pupils can attend your school from the area of another LEA.

7. It is up to a parent to ensure that a pupil gets to school regularly and on time, so a longish journey for the child is not in itself a reason for not admitting him or her. However, if the child is likely to arrive dog-tired every day because of an early start, it would not be good for the child to come to your school.

8. You could reasonably use a family connection as a criterion for admission. Perhaps a father, mother or sibling attends or attended the school.

9. You should avoid all reference to a rigid catchment area. Commonsense suggests that to have one at all is to kill off the very choice for parents which Parliament intended to create. You might, however, give preference to pupils from a particular school: LEAs often do this by referring to 'designated schools'. This might mean for example that children from your primary school have places 'designated' for them in a particular secondary school. This does not mean any more than 'reserved for them if they want them'.

Watch this one, though. It is common for parents nowadays to select a secondary school and then send their son or daughter to one of its feeder primary schools to make sure of a place at the secondary of their choice. Carried to its conclusion this could mean that parents who might choose your school at the secondary stage lose their choice. You should take this into account in your planning. Too rigid adherence to the principle of 'designation' might be unreasonable.

From what has been said above it's clear that your head should not have operated a waiting list but should have left matters to the governors or Appeal Panel.

Problem Several parents and neighbours at your school have complained about the apparent lack of control and poor behaviour of pupils at lunchtime. It is said that pupils wander around the vicinity of the school in gangs getting up to all sorts of mischief and occasionally vandalism. There never seems to be anyone around to control the pupils.

Comment This remains one of the most difficult unresolved problems in school management.

At one time LEAs were obliged by law to have a school meals service in all their schools. The LEA provided the kitchen staff and food, and the head and his colleagues supervised the serving of the meal and the welfare of the pupils. Those on duty were entitled to a free meal.

The 1980 Education Act made the school meals service optional for LEAs: most have continued, although often in a modified form. The only legal requirement now is that children from poorer families must be given free 'refreshment' at lunchtime and facilities must be provided for children who wish to bring something to eat at lunchtime.

The teachers' contract, however, (see p. 190) does not require them to supervise at lunchtime, and fewer and fewer now volunteer to do so. It would be quite wrong to assume, however, that this means that they do nothing: a glance into your staffroom will show them getting ready for the afternoon, running clubs and marking work.

To replace the help formerly given at lunchtime by teachers, LEA employ the so-called 'dinner ladies' or 'welfare assistants'. The disciplinary problems at your school probably arise in part because, with the best will in the world, and kind-hearted as most of them are, the dinner ladies simply don't have teachers' expertise in handling large groups of children, probably spread out over a large unfenced campus.

The head is in a very difficult position now. His contract requires him to see that all is well at lunchtime. For heads who have inadequate backup from the welfare assistants this can mean that they have to be around every lunchtime until retirement or death (and many heads see it in just that light!). Even worse, in some schools the fact that the head is the only 'heavyweight' professional around leads to a situation that even he cannot handle satisfactorily. In many schools the first part of afternoon class time is spent by teachers in sorting out disciplinary problems which have arisen at lunchtime.

Here are a few ideas for easing the problem which heads and governors up and down the country have worked out:

1. Use gentle persuasion on parents to see if you can reduce the numbers staying for lunch. This eases the burden on the dinner helpers: with fewer to look after things can only get better. Spell out to parents just what the situation at lunchtime is, and enlist their support.

2. Press the LEA to provide more dinner helpers. Clearly spell out the consequences of a full-scale riot at lunchtime.

3. Shorten the lunch break. The norm has been traditionally about 90 minutes, but many schools have got it down to about 50. This reduces the opportunity for mischief! Remember, though, to consult parents and the LEA carefully about this as school will finish earlier in the afternoon.

4. Try a 'shift system' for school meals. Half the children eat say from 12.00–12.45 while the others remain in class being taught. The other half eats from 12.45–13.30. This means that no more than half the school at any one time is away from the supervision of teachers.

5. If the problem centres on a few pupils only, the law will support you in taking disciplinary action. The head can ban them from the school at lunchtime, or in severe cases you can exclude. Newton's First Law of The Perverse always seems to operate in that there may be the sad case of one pupil being on free school meals in the group which has been excluded. The law makes no exception however.

6. If the situation is really bad at lunchtime you should carefully consider whether to close the school, giving notice to the parents first, of course. If the best advice available to you is that there is a grave foreseeable risk to life and limb you probably have the *duty* to close down. Parents may grumble about the lack of a lunch: they would grumble even more if their children were injured.

It is worth noting if you have such an extreme situation in your school that the 1980 Act does not require children from poorer families to be given a full meal: the Act talks of 'refreshment'. Nor does the Act require this to be given on school premises. A good quality packed lunch would probably satisfy the law. Take this up with your LEA. You could, of course, if you wished make an exception for these children, but this is not necessarily what their parents would wish.

He's always late to school!

Problem Joe Slack persistently arrives at school anything up to half an hour late. His father says that the boy doesn't walk very quickly, has to walk nearly three miles and can't go the shortest way because that means crossing a dangerous main road. He can't afford the bus fare and is not going to do anything about his son's attendance until the LEA or governors provide a free bus pass. In any case, he wanted Joe to go to St Ignatius RC School about ten miles away but the LEA had refused to give him a buss pass for that too.

The head is thinking about excluding Joe from school because he is setting a bad example to other pupils.

Comment First, it is not the responsibility of the school to enforce attendance at school by disciplinary action of this sort, although it is generally expected that teachers will make reasonable grumbling noises to pupils and their parents about lateness and absence and give appropriate nudges. The law puts the responsibility of enforcement squarely onto the LEA. The school notifies the LEA about absences and leaves it at that. So avoid going down the exclusion road.

Secondly, the law regards lateness as absence. Parents of children at school must ensure 'regular attendance', which the law defines as attendance for the full time the school is open. Pupils who arrive late (there is usually a margin of about 15–20 minutes tolerance) are marked in class registers as absent.

The question of distance and free transport is a bit more complex nowadays. Children under eight must face a walk of over two miles to school before they become eligible for free transport: over eight, the distance increases to three miles so Joe is not eligible.

Until recently the law took the view that the distance from home to school was measured by 'the nearest available route'. If that route perhaps was along a public right of way over a muddy field, the law took the view that parents should buy Wellingtons for their children, not condone them arriving late by sending them a long way round. Nor could parents claim a free travel pass by sending their children to school down a longer route.

The LEA can decide that the 'nearest available route' for a child is too dangerous, and can provide transport if the safer route is over the limits on distance. However, it is up to the LEA to decide whether the route is dangerous, not Joe's father, no matter how strongly he feels.

Similarly it is up to the LEA to decide whether it is prepared to give Joe a bus pass to attend St Ignatius. Most LEAs are happy to provide free transport if parents choose a denominational school for their child, but, strictly speaking, have done their legal duty by offering Joe a place in his present school.

The boring headteacher's report

Problem At your governors' meeting much time is always spent in listening to the headteacher's report. It always describes in great detail what has happened since the last meeting. The chair always invites the head to read the report – perhaps he thinks you're illiterate? You begin to wonder whether your headteacher spins all this out until everyone has gone home in despair!

Comment Two common difficulties are, first, that the report is all about past history. Knowing what has already happened is necessary and interesting but gives governors no chance to influence future policy beyond perhaps saying 'Let's not do so-and-so again'. Second, if the relationship between the head and governors is not as open and confident as it should be, it allows the head to keep out tricky issues which the governors would prefer to have discussed. And if governors have heard about some issue outside the school and it does not appear in the report, there is immediately an unfortunate feeling at the meeting that someone has been caught out.

The head too may find the report a bore. After all, he knows all too well that the girls' under-14 netball team was beaten by the Gasworks View lot last week, and dwelling on it is no fun for anyone.

There are no local or national rules or regulations about what the head's report should contain. Some LEAs have guidelines for the benefit of newly appointed heads, but these are only suggestions and governors can agree with their head to have the report written in any way they like.

There are a number of ways of overcoming the difficulties mentioned above. Reports can be produced in two parts, the first being 'Matters for discussion' and the second 'Routine items of information'. The disaster of the girls' netball result would come into the latter. The chairman expects governors to have read Part 2 before the meeting and starts by asking if anyone particularly wants an item from Part 2 to be moved to 'Matters for discussion'.

The chairman may discuss with the head before the meeting just what the 'Matters for discussion' are to be. The governors too may have decided at a previous meeting that such and such a matter should be discussed, and have perhaps asked the head to prepare a report in advance of the meeting.

Most important, the head's report should contain a section on future policy, since this is an important way in which governors can bring influence to bear. If governors read for example, that 'Mr Trickey (Maths) resigned with effect from the end of the summer term, and was replaced by Mrs Solvit', they have lost an important opportunity. The head would have known that Mr Trickey was looking for a job elsewhere, because the head would have been asked to write references or had seen a letter of resignation. Had the governors also been told they could have discussed in good time whether to use the opportunity of a staff vacancy to staff another subject in the school, or possibly in this case to introduce, say, computer studies. If governors leave the policy on staff appointments to the head, they cut themselves off from real influence on the curriculum.

Similarly, governors need to be informed in advance of the number of pupils likely to be in the school in the coming year, in case reorganization is on the horizon; of the likelihood that public examination results will not be so good next summer; of the fact that pupils who want to study Spanish in the sixth form next year will not be able to do so because the only teacher of Spanish is needed to spend all her time teaching the first and second forms. These are just a few examples of where knowledge gained in good time can help governors to play a constructive role in the affairs of their school.

8

Now that you're
a good school governor

There is more to being a successful school governor than reading a book about it. On the other hand your willingness to learn about schools, children, curriculum, teachers and the duties of school governors by reading this book is a very healthy sign of interest and goodwill.

The quiz below is mainly lighthearted, but also slightly serious. It is certainly not a properly validated test, merely a set of questions about being a governor. In each section there are five questions. Score one point each time you respond (hand on heart!) 'yes', or give a correct answer which can be verified from local knowledge or reference to this book.

If you score 0 or 1 on any section you may need to take positive steps to improve your knowledge and effectiveness in that area. If you score 4 or 5 you are quite possibly very good at that aspect of your job as a governor. Alternatively you may be a dab hand at magazine quizzes, lucky, or a bit of a fibber.

A Curriculum

1 Have you read any curriculum statement the school or LEA may have prepared in recent years?

2 Do you know if the school operates through separate

subjects or on blocks of time for integrated project and topic work or both (primary)?

or Do you know if the school teaches subjects like Biology, Chemistry, Physics, History, Geography, separately or through integrated fields like combined science and humanities (secondary)?

3 Do you know what scheme, if any, is used for number work or mathematics in your school (primary)?

or Do you know what choices are available to children at the 'options' stage (secondary)?

4 Do you know what the school does for children who are exceptionally able or who learn more slowly?

5 Could you say what the school is doing to deal with new technology such as micro-electronics and the micro-computer?

B Teachers and teaching

1 Have you talked to any teachers in the school about their views on current issues in education?

2 Do you know what sort of in-service courses teachers in the school have been attending?

3 Have you talked informally to the head about life in the school and about matters such as teacher appraisal?

4 Do you know how teachers monitor and assess pupils' progress?

5 Have you asked teachers what difficulties they may be facing or what they may need to do their job more effectively?

C Parents and Community

1 Have you ever asked parents what they like or dislike about the school?

2 Have you ever attended a parents' meeting?

3 Have you visited different parts of the school's catchment area?

4 Do you know what jobs parents in the area do or what level of unemployment there is?

5 Are you familiar with any use made of the school outside normal hours by members of the community?

D Children

1 Have you talked to any children in the school (other than your own if you are a parent governor)?

2 Have you been to watch any of the children's plays, concerts or sports?

3 Have you looked at any of the children's work, either on display or anywhere else?

4 Do you know how the school handles children with learning or behaviour problems?

5 Do you know what leisure interests children in the school enjoy?

E Organization

1 Do you know how decisions are made in the school about policy and curriculum?

2 Do you know the names of your fellow governors?

3 Have you ever attended a meeting of the education committee?

4 Could you understand a simple financial statement about your school's budget?

5 Would you know how to get an item put on the agenda of your governors' meeting?

F Action

1 If an urgently needed building project were continually deferred, would you know what action to take?

2 Are you willing to 'get things moving' if governors' meetings become tedious or pointless?

3 If your school were threatened with closure, would you know what to do?

4 Have you ever volunteered to do anything at a governors' meeting?

5 Do you tend to participate in most meetings and not continually defer to the head or chairman?

Scores (out of 5)	Points
A Curriculum	....
B Teachers and Teaching	....
C Parents and Community	....
D Children	....
E Organization	....
F Action	....
TOTAL	

Total score

25–30 You must frighten the life out of your fellow governors, the head and staff with your knowledge and energy. Do you ever sleep, pause for breath, say hello to the budgie or your family, or for that matter, tell the truth in magazine quizzes?

18–24 Congratulations, you are a black belt governor. Two or three like you and the local authority will go bankrupt because your school will get all the resources.

7–17 You are probably strong in some sections of the quiz and weaker in others. See if you need to work at aspects where you obtained a low score.

1–6 If you are a new governor you have probably not yet had time to learn about the school, but if you have been a governor for several years, ask yourself how you can be more effective.

0 Resign, but only after checking your pulse. You may have passed away at a boring governors' meeting and been allowed to stay on posthumously.

Appendix A
What do teachers do all day?

In many trades and professions the trend nowadays is towards giving employees fairly detailed descriptions of the work they are paid to do.

Teachers have traditionally resisted this. They have seen themselves rather more as additional parents to children, doing what parents do as the need arises. Because of this, schools and children have benefited enormously from the vast number of out-of-school activities such as foreign journeys, plays, evening concerts, Saturday football which teachers have been keen to offer. Parents do not have a detailed 'job description', so neither do teachers, ran the argument.

However, in recent years the teaching profession has been subjected to a number of pressures which have conspired to change the climate in schools. More and more work has been piled onto schools by society at large, by parents (sometimes governors too!) occasionally taking too much for granted, and not least by the DES and LEAs eager for curriculum change. Few would deny that schools nowadays are far more stressful places than they were only a few years ago.

Also as in many walks of life, salaries have become a sore point with teachers, but rather as 'the last straw' rather than the only bone of contention. During the 1980s teachers discovered that they could take effective disruptive action in schools by refusing to carry out parts of the job: LEAs and heads were unable to counteract this effectively to keep schools running smoothly because there was no firm contractual arrangement with their teachers about just what the job included. Questions were asked such as: Could a teacher be required to attend staff meetings outside normal working hours? Was a teacher entitled to a break at lunchtime and to leave the premises? Could a teacher be required to spend evenings rehearsing a school play? and so on. Many readers may be surprised that there were no clear answers to questions like this — and perhaps even more surprised that teachers had no legal entitlement to holidays (other than Public Holidays) either! The position in law was actually that teachers were employed to work for the full year, but that from time to time their employers chose to shut down the workplace and send the children away, so that there was less for teachers to do!

The position since 1987 is that all teachers in maintained schools work to a detailed contract which was drawn up and enforced by the DES. Under schemes of local financial management (see p. 27) governors need to know something about the contract because they are, to all intents and purposes, employers. The contract does not apply incidentally to teachers in non-maintained ('Public') schools, for one reason because the needs of boarding schools are different. The full text of the teachers' job description is reproduced on pp. 192–6. Some important things to know about it are:

1. Teachers can be required to work for no more than 1265 hours each year. This is roughly a 36-hour week. These are long hours when compared with those of teachers in continental Europe, where salaries are also much higher. They are also now guaranteed five days every year for further professional training.

2. Preparation of school work, report writing, marking and so on, insofar as it cannot be done within the 1265 hours, must be done in teachers' own time. Teachers, particularly in primary schools, have little time for preparation during school hours.

3. Teachers now work to 'directed' and 'self-directed' time. The former is work given to them by the head and comes out of the 1265 hours. The latter is work which teachers undertake to do voluntarily.

4. The head has to ensure that the basic demands of the school

on each teacher are fitted into the 1265 hours. This includes staff meetings, supervision time (morning break supervision, for example), teaching, parents' evenings and other necessary activities. Most heads now operate a 'time budget' within their school. It might lay down for example:

School year 1988/89

Parents' evenings: 6 at 2 hours each = 12 hours p.a.

Full staff meetings: 9 at 1 hour each = 9 hours p.a.

Departmental staff meetings: These will count as directed time only if agreed in advance with the head: maximum 10 hours p.a.

Case conferences out of school about pupils with problems: maximum 2 hours each.

Readers will spot immediately that these arrangements are not helpful when it comes to out-of-school activities. No head in his right mind would let his two teachers of German take a group to Germany for ten days on 'directed time'. The teachers on such journeys, like parents, are on duty for 24 hours a day, so the teachers would consume 240 of their 1265 hours very quickly indeed. German classes at the school might then have to stop at Easter! In the same way it would be unwise of any head to give an open cheque to any teacher to spend as many hours as the teacher might choose in rehearsing a play. No-one knows precisely what would happen if a head were unfortunate enough to run out of hours. The LEA might have to move in other teachers for the rest of the year. (They wouldn't be too fond of you and your head as managers, either.)

Governing bodies should keep themselves informed about the 'time budget' for their school. It is, however, the head's job to set it up and keep it running smoothly.

SCHEDULE 3

CONDITIONS OF EMPLOYMENT
OF SCHOOL TEACHERS

Exercise of general professional duties

1. A teacher who is not a head teacher shall carry out the professional duties of a school teacher as circumstances may require
> (a) if he is employed as a teacher in a school, under the reasonable direction of the head teacher of that school;
> (b) if he is employed by an authority on terms under which he is not assigned to any one school, under the reasonable direction of that authority and of the head teacher of any school in which he may for the time being be required to work as a teacher.

Exercise of particular duties

2. (a) A teacher employed as a teacher (other than a head teacher) in a school shall perform, in accordance with any directions which may reasonably be given to him by the head teacher from time to time, such particular duties as may reasonably be assigned to him;
> (b) A teacher employed by an authority on terms such as those described in paragraph 1(b) above shall perform, in accordance with any direction which may reasonably be given to him from time to time by the authority or by the head teacher of any school in which he may for the time being be required to work as a teacher, such particular duties as may reasonably be assigned to him.

Professional duties

3. The following duties shall be deemed to be included

in the professional duties which a school teacher may be required to perform

Teaching (1)(a) Planning and preparing courses and lessons;

(b) Teaching, according to their educational needs, the pupils assigned to him, including the setting and marking of work to be carried out by the pupil in school and elsewhere;

(c) Assessing, recording and reporting on the development, progress and attainment of pupils;

Other activities (2)(a) Promoting the general progress and well being of individual pupils and of any class or group of pupils assigned to him;

(b) Providing guidance and advice to pupils on educational and social matters and on their further education and future careers, including information about sources of more expert advice on specific questions: making relevant records and reports;

(c) Making records and reports on the personal and social needs of pupils;

(d) Communicating and consulting with the parents of pupils;

(e) Communicating and co-operating with persons or bodies outside the school;

(f) Participating in meetings arranged for any of the purposes described above;

Assessments and reports (3) Providing or contributing to oral and written assessments, reports and references relating to individual pupils and groups of pupils;

Appraisal (4) Participating in any arrangement within an agreed national framework for the appraisal of his performance and that of other teachers;

Review; Further training and development (5)(a) Reviewing from time to time his methods of teaching and programmes of work;

(b) Participating in arrangements for his further training and professional development as a teacher;

Educational methods (6) Advising and co-operating with the head teacher and other teachers (or any one or more of them) on the preparation and development of courses of study, teaching materials, teaching programmes, methods of teaching and assessment and pastoral arrangements;

Discipline, health and safety

(7) Maintaining good order and discipline among the pupils and safeguarding their health and safety both when they are authorized to be on the school premises and when they are engaged in authorized school activities elsewhere;

Staff Meetings

(8) Participating in meetings at the school which relate to the curriculum for the school or the administration or organization of the school, including pastoral arrangements;

Cover

(9) Supervising and so far as practicable teaching any pupils whose teacher is not available to teach them;
Provided that no teacher shall be required to provide such cover—

(a) after the teacher who is absent or otherwise not available has been so for three or more consecutive working days; or

(b) where the fact that the teacher would be absent or otherwise not available for a period exceeding three consecutive working days was known to the maintaining authority for two or more working days before the absence commenced;

unless

(i) he is a teacher employed wholly or mainly for the purpose of providing such cover ('a supply teacher'); or

(ii) it is not reasonably practicable for the maintaining authority to provide a supply teacher to provide cover; or

(iii) he is a full-time teacher at the school but has been assigned by the head teacher in the time-table to teach or carry out other specified duties (except cover) for less than 75 per cent of those hours in the week during which pupils are taught at the school;

Public examinations

(10) Participating in arrangements for preparing pupils for public examinations and in assessing pupils for the purposes of such examinations; recording and reporting such assessments; and participating in arrangements for pupils' presentation for and supervision during such examinations;

Management

(11)(a) Contributing to the selection for appointment and professional development of other teachers and non-teaching staff, including the induction and assessment of new and probationary teachers;

(b) Co-ordinating or managing the work of other teachers;

(c) Taking such part as may be required of him in the review, development and management of activities relating to the curriculum, organization and pastoral functions of the school;

Administration (12)(a) Participating in administrative and organizational tasks related to such duties as are described above, including the management or supervision of persons providing support for the teachers in the school and the ordering and allocation of equipment and materials;

(b) Attending assemblies, registering the attendance of pupils and supervising pupils, whether these duties are to be performed before, during or after school sessions.

Working time

4.(1) After 1st August 1987–

(a) a teacher employed full-time, other than in the circumstances described in subparagraph (c), shall be available for work for 195 days in any year, of which 190 days shall be days on which he may be required to teach pupils in addition to carrying out other duties; and those 195 days shall be specified by his employer or, if the employer so directs, by the head teacher;

(b) a teacher shall be available to perform such duties at such times and such places as may be specified by the head teacher (or, where the teacher is not assigned to any one school, by his employer or the head teacher of any school in which he may for the time being be required to work as a teacher) for 1265 hours in any year, those hours to be allocated reasonably throughout those days in the year on which he is required to be available for work;

(c) subparagraphs (a) and (b) do not apply to a teacher employed wholly or mainly to teach or perform other duties in relation to pupils in a residential establishment;

(d) time spent in travelling to and from the place of work shall not count against the 1265 hours referred to in subparagraph (b);

(e) unless employed under a separate contract as a midday supervisor, a teacher shall not be required to undertake midday supervision, and shall be allowed a break of reasonable length either between school sessions or between the hours of 12 noon and 2.00 pm;

(f) a teacher shall, in addition to the requirements set out in subparagraphs (a) and (b) above, work such additional hours as may be needed to enable him to discharge effectively his professional duties, including, in particular the marking of pupils' work, the writing of reports on pupils and the preparation of lessons, teaching material and teaching programmes. The amount of time required for this purpose beyond the 1265 hours referred to in subparagraph (b) and the times outside the 1265 specified hours at which duties shall be performed shall not be defined by the employer but shall depend upon the work needed to discharge the teacher's duties;

(2) In this paragraph, 'year' means a period of 12 months commencing on 1st September unless the school's academic year begins in August in which case it means a period of 12 months commencing on 1st August.

Appendix B

Sample primary and secondary school budgets

A sample primary school budget
(from *Local Financial Management in Schools*, Peat, Marwick, McLintock, Longman, 1988).

The LFM budget of Buckden Primary School (300 Pupils), Cambridgeshire, 1987–88, as at July, 1987

Cambridgeshire LFM scheme – Schools   * 318 * 01/08/87
Expenditure and Income
for the period ended July 1987   468 Buckden C of E CT

	Revised total budget for year £	Expected to date £	Actual to date £	Variation to date £
Employees				
0110 Full time teachers	173,898	58,255	56,913.92	1,341.08−
0112 Casual supply teachers	2,207	789	241.98	547.02−
0120 Support staff	8,661	2,767	2,865.27	98.27
0141 Caretakers	6,510	2,127	1,358.55	768.45−
0142 Cleaners	2,890	999	1,740.17	741.17
	194,166	64,937	63,119.89	1,817.11−

	Revised total budget for year £	Expected to date £	Actual to date £	Variation to date £
Premises				
1320 Oil	2,239	799	452.00	347.00−
1330 Electricity	2,000	560	381.01	178.99−
1340 Gas-mains	60	20	18.95	1.05−
1351 Water charges	663	243	187.88	55.12−
1360 Cleaning materials	417	124	330.22	206.22
1370 Window cleaning	60	20	0.00	20.00−
1391 Refuse collection	188	63	180.39	117.39
1540 General rates	10,597	3,179	5,416.37	2,237.37
1541 Sewerage rates	537	197	228.08	31.08
	16,761	5,205	7,194.90	1,989.90
Supplies & services				
2600 Capitation allowances	8,490	2,428	1,243.71	1,184.29−
	8,490	2,428	1,243.71	1,184.29−
Transport & Mvble Pl				
3110 Car allowances	374	124	572.30	448.30
	374	124	572.30	448.30
Establishment expenses				
4040 Advertising for staff	205	69	105.09	36.09
4120 Candidates exps	4	1	68.60	67.60
	209	70	173.69	103.69
Miscellaneous Exps				
Total Expenditure	220,000	72,764	72,304.49	459.51−
Income				
8420 Casual lettings	20−	7−	15.60−	8.60−
8421 Ctkrs/clnrs etc. fees	50−	16−	21.60−	5.60−
8422 Heat & light charge	20−	6−	15.60−	9.60−
	90−	29−	52.80−	23.80−

	Revised total budget for year £	Expected to date £	Actual to date £	Variation to date £
Net Expenditure	219,910	72,735	72,251.69	483.31−

A sample secondary school budget

Budget Proposals

	1987/88	*1988/89*
TUITION ACCOUNTS	£	£
Teachers' salaries	863,775	936,750
National Insurance	56,250	65,500
Superannuation	80,500	84,350
Prizes	650	650
Textbooks	8,200	2,500
Stationery	1,250	2,750
Physics	3,590	3,576
Chemistry	3,835	3,810
Biology	5,735	3,310
Lab. technicians' wages	30,160	32,000
Art & Design	21,292	22,036
Mathematics	1,270	2,137
English	2,600	2,497
Modern Languages	2,012	880
History	1,185	2,822
Economics	1,000	750
Classics	151	617
Geography/Geology	1,527	2,272
Music, Instruments, Sundries	5,770	6,200
Religious Studies	980	1,074
Games & Swimming	5,697	6,200
Team Travel	5,500	7,000
Library	3,000	3,000
Drama Society	1,750	1,750
Other activities & societies	5,000	5,500
Junior School	968	1,007
Classroom furniture & equipment	3,750	4,000
Acad. depts printing & stationery	8,500	9,500
School brochure	1,000	1,000
Examination expenses	500	750
Maint. of classroom equipment	4,000	4,000

	1987/88	1988/89
	£	£
Lectures, entertainment, films	1,000	1,100
Technology	3,300	5,945
Business Studies	559	271
General Studies	559	1,696
Information Technology	12,370	5,209
TOTAL	1,642,871	1,991,946

MAINTENANCE ACCOUNTS
Gardens & grounds

	1987/88	1988/89
Wages – gardeners, groundsmen	62,010	65,000
Equipment	2,500	5,000
Repairs to equipment	2,250	4,000
Materials	4,500	6,000
Trees & shrubs	300	300
Contractors charges	1,750	2,000
Sundries	50	50
SUB TOTAL	73,360	82,300

Buildings & equipment

	1987/88	1988/89
Salaries & wages, maintenance staff	42,500	45,000
Materials & equipment	11,500	12,500
Repairs & maint. to plant & equipment	4,750	6,000
Electrical contractor	4,500	5,000
Decorating contractor	15,000	16,000
Plumbing contractor	12,500	12,500
Maint. & cleaning contracts	9,000	10,000
Sundries	50	50
Building contractor	5,000	6,000
Alterations & additions	5,000	6,000
Rolling maintenance expenses	22,250	22.250
SUB TOTAL	132,050	141,300

EXTRAORDINARY EXPENDITURE

	1987/88	1988/89
Renewals, alterations & additions	12,000	15,000
Provision for bad debts from parents	500	500
Sundries & contingencies	*44,000	+61,675
TOTAL	56,500	77,175

* Admin. Mini Computer.	7,000
P.R. & Video.	14,000
Music School Pianos.	23,000

+	P.R. & Printing.	10,000
	In-Service Training	8,000
	Hall Stage Curtains	2,000
	Information Technology	41,675
	TOTAL	125,675

Select bibliography

Books

Barrell, G.R. and Partington, J.A., *Teachers and the Law* (6th ed.), Methuen, 1985.
    One of the few standard works on the subject, touching on nearly all the legal issues which affect teachers and the education system.
Bennett, Neville, *Teaching Styles and Pupil Progress*, Open Books, 1976.
    A research report into formal and informal teaching styles.
Blanchard, T., Lovell, R., and Ville, N., *Managing Finance in Schools*, Cassell, 1989.
    A guide to the system of school accounting introduced by the Education Act of 1988.
Brooksbank, K. and Anderson, K., *School Governors* (2nd ed.), Longman, 1987.
    A very useful and detailed reference book, written by two Chief Education Officers of wide experience. It contains a glossary of the sometimes baffling terms bandied about at governors' meetings.
Burgess, T. and Sofer, A., *The School Governors' Handbook and Training Guide*, Kogan Page, 1986.
    Slightly dry in style but packaged with valuable information.
Desforges, C., *Testing and Assessment*, Cassell, 1989.

An introduction to the subject for parents and others interested.

Griffiths, Alex and Hamilton, Dorothy, *Parent, Teacher, Child*, Methuen, 1984.

—— *Learning at Home*, Methuen Children's Books, 1987.
These two books give a clear and readable introduction to the PACT scheme, which is a venture in parent/teacher co-operation in primary schools. The first book is addressed to teachers, the second to parents.

Jones, A., *Leadership for Tomorrow's Schools*, Blackwell, 1987.
Contains, among other things, a depressing account of a survey of 500 secondary school heads in which they revealed frankly what they thought of their governors. Not a lot, it must be said! Things to be learned here.

Kogan, M., *School Governing Bodies*, Heinemann, 1984.
A survey of what governing bodies actually do and what governors think of them. Academic in tone but useful background reading.

Lowe, C., *The Education Act 1986*, pub. Secondary Heads' Association, 197 St Paul's Road, London N1 2NB.
A very useful and concise commentary, written by a highly experienced head. Good on the effects of the Act on the day-to-day running of schools.

Mahoney, T., *Governing Schools: Powers, Issues and Practice*, Macmillan Education, 1988.
The author is involved with school governor training in Leicestershire. There are particularly helpful sections on race relations and equal opportunity legislation, and the author tackles some controversial issues like sex education in schools.

Partington, J.A., *Law and the New Teacher*, Holt-Saunders, 1984.
An easy-to-read introduction to the subject for new teachers.

Pring, R.A., *The New Curriculum*, Cassell, 1989.
A comprehensive account of the curriculum for children from 5–18. Discusses the National Curriculum and the issues underlying the construction of a school curriculum.

Sallis, J., *Questions Governors Ask*, Advisory Centre for Education, 1984.

—— *The Effective School Governor*, Advisory Centre for Education, 1980.

—— *Schools, Parents and Governors: A New Approach to Account-ability*, Routledge, 1988.

The author is known nationally as one of Britain's most active and experienced school governors and has written widely on the subject. Highly recommended reading.

Wragg, E.C. and Partington, J.A., *Schools and Parents*, Cassell, 1989.

An easy-to-read introduction to the education system and current issues, for parents.

Periodicals and booklets

ACE Bulletin

The Advisory Centre for Education's bi-monthly magazine is very useful reading for school governors and those interested in education generally.

ACE, 18 Victoria Park Square, London E2 9PB.

Department of Education and Science booklets

The following are all obtainable free of charge from: DES Publications Despatch Centre, Canons Park, Honeypot Lane, Stanmore, Middx HA7 1AZ.

School Governors, 1988

An outline of the changes in school government introduced during 1986 and 1988.

Local Management of Schools, 1988

A report on local financial management of schools, commissioned by the DES from Coopers and Lybrand, an independent firm of financial consultants. An interesting insight into the background of delegated budgets for schools.

Education

Available weekly from newsagents. Very readable, highly authoritative and widely read in LEA circles.

School Governor

A very informative and well-produced quarterly magazine of interest to all governors. Available from:

6/7 Hockley Hill, Hockley, Birmingham B18 5AA.

Times Educational Supplement

Probably the most widely-read weekly newspaper in this field. Available from your newsagent.

Other resources

Governors' Basic Training Pack
Very useful. Available from:
National Association of Governors and Managers, 10
Brookfield Park, London NW5 1ER.
Peat, Marwick, McLintock, *Local Financial Management in Schools*,
Longman, 1988.
A familiarization and initial training pack for those coming
fresh to delegated school budgets.

Index

207